D1607885

Selling Higher, Broader and Deeper:

How to Successfully Navigate to the C-Suite and Beyond

DENNIS FALCI

AND

RON LAMBERT

Selling Higher, Broader and Deeper: How to Successfully Navigate to the C-Suite and Beyond

© 2020 YUKON TRAINING

Dedications:

DENNIS FALCI:

To my wife, Carrie, and our two sons, Derek and Devin. Thank you for your love and support. You inspire me every day. I could not have asked for better teammates in life than you.

RON LAMBERT:

This book is dedicated to salespeople all over the world who strive every day to help their customers succeed. I consider myself blessed to have worked with so many thousands of these professionals over almost 50 years of my sales career. I am always amazed at the courage and endurance of professional salespeople who never, ever quit. They are the reason for successful businesses everywhere, as they always pursue the goal that they have been given or set themselves. Press on! I also dedicate this book to my best friend and wife of 50 years, Debbie. Simply said, she is an incredible person, wife, mother and grandmother.

Table of Contents

About the Authors

Dennis Falci is the President and Owner of Yukon Training, Inc., a professional development and consulting firm headquartered in Cedar Knolls, New Jersey. For over 30 years, Yukon has been assisting organizations achieve their goals of selling higher, broader and deeper through Yukon's blended learning approach of live skill set training through customized workshops.

Prior to joining Yukon, Dennis served as the Director of Market Access Training for 8 years with Sanofi, a pharmaceutical company based in Bridgewater, New Jersey. He was responsible for training Account Executives and Field Sales Professionals. During this time, the Account Management team was often listed in the top three in the industry for companies calling on insurers and pharmacy benefit management (PBM) organizations. He also handled all skill set training for the organization.

Dennis was with Sanofi for almost 23 years. Prior to becoming the Director of Market Access Training, he held numerous positions within the organization, including Senior Manager of Marketing, where he was responsible for developing and launching non-branded tools and tactics for the account management team to assist in vertical and horizontal integration within accounts; and Regional Account Manager, where he called higher, broader and deeper on Insurers, PBMs, group purchasing organizations (GPOs), medical groups and hospital systems. Before this, he served as District Sales Manager, Institutional Sales Representative and Sales Professional.

During his tenure with Sanofi, Dennis received numerous awards of merit, including Sales Representative of the Year, Account Manager of the Year, Account Team of the Year (Team Leader), Marketing

Champion of the Year finalist and Best Account Manager selected by his customers for 4 consecutive years.

He currently serves on the Leadership Advisory Council for Seton Hall University and has been a member of a panel of assessors for the Seton Hall University School of Business since 2000. He and his wife, Carrie, reside in New Jersey and have 2 sons and a rescue dog.

Ron Lambert founded Yukon Training in 1989 after serving as National Director of Customer Relations for A.H. Robins and as Executive Vice President for Data Systems. At A.H. Robins, Ron called on the company's top 20 customers, often at the C-Suite level. He served on numerous industry committees including the Executive Advisory Board for the National Wholesale Druggists Association. In his role at Data Systems, Ron often met monthly with customer CEOs in one-on-one situations. Throughout his nearly 50 years of sales experience, he has conducted over a thousand executive calls. He has also conducted hundreds of Selling Higher courses throughout the United States, Canada, France, the United Kingdom and the United Arab Emirates.

He is no stranger to corporate boardrooms, as he has served on a number of corporate boards and is a board member and/or chairman for non-profits such as the Better Business Bureau; the YMCA; the Mathews Community Foundation; PATH, Inc.; and the Mathews Volunteer Rescue Squad. These experiences plus his rich understanding of business acumen have enabled him to develop unique approaches of how to sell higher, broader and deeper in both medium-sized and large corporate settings.

He is also the co-author of Is That Your Hand in My Pocket?: The Sales Professional's Guide to Negotiating. Ron resides in the rural community of Mathews, Virginia, near the Chesapeake Bay.

Acknowledgements

We would like to thank the following individuals; without whose assistance this book would not have been possible:

John Kirwan, for his assistance with some of the base material for sections of this book. John has been a colleague and friend for many years. Deb Newton, a gifted instructional designer, writer and communication specialist, whose amazing work has made all of Yukon Training's workshops better and who assisted with the layout and flow of this book. Deb has spent over 25 years working with companies to develop curriculum, training and marketing materials that meet the needs of her customers. Chris Ayers, former owner of Yukon Training who had the vision of putting together a white paper on selling higher, broader and deeper. You can read many of the findings of that paper in this book. Tom Parker and Mark Moyer, excellent facilitators who bring to life the content in this book in Yukon's Selling Higher workshop. Lara Gallo, a master of organization who helps to keep us all in line. Maura Logue and Tara Myzie, for their work to edit and design this book, respectively. Our families, without whose ongoing support, love and dedication this book simply would have remained a dream and not become a reality.

Selling is Difficult ...

... , especially if you are meeting with the "wrong" customers or finding it difficult to get in front of the "right" customers.

There is no doubt that the customers you currently meet with are important to your business, yet what if there were other people in the same organization that could increase your level of influence within an organization? Would you want to meet with them?

For many, the answer is "of course I would," but then the doubts come in:

> "What if I mess up my current relationships?"
>
> "What if I have nothing to present to 'those' people?"
>
> "Why would they want to meet with me?"
>
> "What value can I bring?"

The other questions you could ask yourself might be:

> "Would I like to make MORE MONEY?"
>
> "Would I like to make my boss and their boss HAPPIER?"
>
> "Would I like to make my current business relationships STRONGER?"
>
> "Would I like to make my selling time and efforts more PRODUCTIVE?"

FOR THESE ANSWERS AND MORE, TURN THE PAGE!

What You Need to Know about Executives and Senior Management

INTRODUCTION

Sam Carter had just made his first cup of coffee before moving to his computer early Monday morning to check his email. The first email immediately caught his eye, as it was marked URGENT and was from his sales manager. He noticed before he opened it that it was sent at 11:18 p.m. on Sunday night and the subject line was "New Initiative!!" "Oh no!" was his first thought, and it got worse as he started reading the email. It said…

● ● ◉

○ ▱ ✓ ✕

Subject: PATH International, Inc.

Sam,

We can talk when I return in 2 weeks, as I'm catching a plane to Indy and then I'm taking a few days off. I received a long phone call late yesterday evening from our new VP of Sales, Devin West. Among other things, he wants an update by the end of the month on what levels we have penetrated at PATH International, Inc. I know that you just took over this account so when I return, let's talk about where you are and develop a plan.

Victoria

"So, another new initiative from a Senior Manager," Sam thought to himself. "Oh well, I have got to get ready for my first call today, so I'll worry about this later."

After getting in his car and heading out to his appointment, within 15 minutes he ran into a massive traffic jam on the Inner Loop. As he was sitting there listening to his radio, he began thinking about that email. Although he had five years of sales experience and had always done well, he had never even tried to call on anyone other than his normal account contacts. Why would someone want him to go above these friends and acquaintances with whom he already had relationships? Some of them, he remembered, had even told him that they were the decision-makers and he should not talk to others in "their" account. If he did, they told him, he would not be allowed to do any additional business with their organizations. As traffic started moving slowly, Sam realized that he needed some help. A good friend of his, Doug, who was an account manager in the consumer products industry was a "superstar" and might be able to give him some advice. He made a mental note to call Doug that afternoon.

Later that day, after calling him and setting up a time to meet Doug the next morning for an early breakfast, Sam went back to confirming appointments with his normal contacts.

In the breakfast meeting with Doug the next day, he soon discovered that he had a lot to learn. Doug laid out how he approached his larger accounts with a methodical, strategic approach that soon had Sam's head spinning.

Explaining the sales methods he uses, Doug gave Sam this first bit of advice: "In every account that has a number of managerial levels, approach the account with the strategy of selling higher, broader and deeper."

At first, Sam was not sure of what Doug meant, but Sam perked up when Doug mentioned that *selling higher means meeting and speaking with Executives and Senior Managers in a particular area or department within an organization. Selling broader is selling across areas or departments within an organization or selling horizontally. Selling deeper, is selling to others within the same area or department or selling vertically.*

"This sounds exactly what I need to," Sam said to Doug, "but I won't be able to do this in my accounts because they will cut me off at the knees!" Doug assured Sam that if he handles these situations correctly, he can actually make his current account relationships stronger.

Doug had made an impression on Sam, and Sam wanted more — a lot more! As he continued to question Doug more, Doug finally said "Sam, I have got to get to work but when I get to my desk, I'm going to send you a lot more information from a company that taught me most of this information. Read it, study it and apply it in small bites and you will never regret the effort you put into this career builder! Before I go, a wise salesperson once told me this, and I have made a lot of money following this advice:

Why sell a trumpet when, with the same effort, you can sell an entire band?

Think about that, Sam: you can do so much more and even have more fun while making a lot of progress in your accounts if you change your approach to one of planning and executing instead of just making calls every day! I'll send you the material and, you can call me once you've digested it and have some questions."

Sam sat in the booth for a few more minutes finishing up his third cup of coffee, thinking about what could be in that information that Doug was going to send him. He was still wondering about it as he got in his car and headed to his first call of the morning.

Later that afternoon, as he entered his house, he threw his bag on the chair by the door and went to his computer. There, three emails down, was a note from Doug with a number of attachments. Doug's note simply said, "Sam, you can do this!"

Here's what Sam read in the attachments:

I think we can all understand why we need to sell higher, yet what has changed that requires us to sell broader and deeper? Decision processes have changed, the complexity of an account has increased, the financial impact of decisions is much more important, regulations are increasing and the number of stakeholders we must interact with has increased. These stakeholders include employees from:

- The C-Suite.
- Quality Control.
- Finance.
- Procurement.
- Sales.
- Marketing.
- Other departments based on the types of accounts you are calling on.

Let's face it, the future of selling within an account can be uncertain.

The benefits of ensuring exposure to all levels of an organization is one way to remain aware of the rapid changes that occur. Staying in touch with people on all levels will ensure you have multiple connections to maintain your foothold within the organization.

Let's begin by examining Executives and Senior Management and how to sell higher to them.

Executives in a company or Senior Management within a department are usually the people that have the most ability to influence the type and amount of business you gain. They are able to provide insight into organizational strategy, are often key decision-makers, and can provide you with connections to others within that organization or other companies within the industry in which you are working.

Of course, meeting with them is more difficult, and they are not often your first point of contact. Executives and Senior Management often have different challenges and concerns than your initial point of contact. That's not to say that they are not aligned; ideally, they are. It's just that they see situations through a different lens and therefore are more engaged when you "speak their language."

Some questions to ask yourself as you look to call on individuals "Higher" within an organization are:
- How do you arrange to meet them?
- Why should you meet with them?
- Why would they want to meet with you?
- Where in the selling process should you meet with them?
- What do you say once you get a meeting?
- Will you provide the same presentation you provided to your initial contact?
- What can you do to ensure you have follow-up meetings?
- How do you establish relationships here without hurting ones at lower levels you have already established?

Before you start trying to get meetings with Executives and Senior Management, there are some facts from a research study Yukon Training, Inc., conducted in concert with Virginia Tech that we want to share. This nationwide study highlights the role that Executives and Senior Managers play in the strategic procurement process in a wide variety of industries and outlines their expectations of sales professionals.

INVOLVEMENT OF THE EXECUTIVE IN THE STRATEGIC PROCUREMENT PROCESS

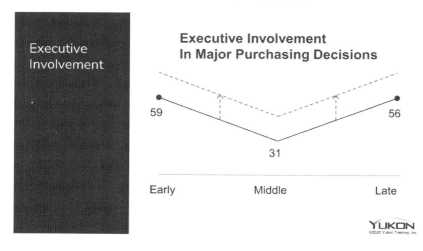

Interviews with Executives and Senior Managers found that:

- Most are involved in the early stages where strategy is developed and objectives established.
- They are least involved in the middle stages where more task-related work is delegated to others and tactics are implemented,
- They are also strongly involved at the later stages of the process, particularly when it comes to measurement of results and ensuring the project was rolled out following their vision.

MANAGED MARKETS DATA FOR PHARMACEUTICALS

Yukon also went back and did additional research within the pharmaceutical industry, surveying managed markets Executives regarding their level of involvement in purchasing decisions.

So given the choice, where is it best for salespeople to enter the process?

Well, it is easiest to enter in the middle; however, Executive involvement is lowest during this stage of the process since vendor selection is usually delegated to others. Also, at this point in the process many organizations are in the formal procurement process, thereby limiting access to Executive stakeholders and usually funneling all communication through a single point of contact within procurement. Salespeople could also choose to wait until later in the process when the Executive reappears; however, selection criteria are usually firmly established and the list of potential candidates narrowed to only a select few that have been vetted along the way.

That leaves the early stage of the process as the best option.

According to this research, Executives and Senior Managers are most likely to devote their time to the following in the early stages:

- Understanding current issues involved in the decision 65%.
- Setting overall strategy 65%.
- Establishing objectives to be met when making the decision 50%.

A CLOSER LOOK AT EXECUTIVE INVOLVEMENT IN THE PROCUREMENT PROCESS

Stage	Item	Percentage
Early	Establishing objectives to be met when making the decision	50%
Early	Understanding current issues involved in the decision	65%
Early	Setting overall strategy	65%
Middle	Exploring options for completing tasks	19%
Middle	Setting criteria for evaluating vendors	27%
Middle	Examining alternative solutions to current plans	31%
Late	Planning the implementation of the project	19%
Late	Measuring results	45%

Executives and Senior Managers are also more receptive to learning about the potential value a new partner could bring to the table in the early stages. For the Executive, the risk is low and the reward potentially high. Objectives and an overall strategy are developed at this stage, and getting "plugged in" to the Executive/Senior Manager at this point can give sales professionals the ability to help influence and shape thinking around these critical items. This stage is also where the procurement process begins taking shape, making access to Executives and Senior Managers and other key stakeholders a little easier.

Our research also uncovered the following:

- Based on current economic conditions, Executive involvement in strategic purchases will increase in the coming years.
- The most effective way to gain access to an Executive continues to be through a referral from someone inside the Executive's own organization.
- A referral from someone outside the organization is the second most effective means of gaining access.
- Responsiveness to questions and requests from Executives is the most effective way for salespeople to differentiate themselves.
- Communication with Executives and other key stakeholders throughout the procurement process can lead to strong consideration for future business, but only if handled appropriately.
- Executives are actively using the internet to research individuals and companies before agreeing to an initial meeting.

PRINCIPLES FOR CALLING ON EXECUTIVES/SENIOR MANAGERS

Never, never, never sell in the C-Suite.

Always have a valid business reason for the call.

Always take into account your current relationships, being careful not to sabotage current relationships for a relationship at a higher level.

Leverage your advocates to gain access to more decision-makers and opportunities.

Make warm calls, rather than cold ones.

Planning the implementation of the project

Develop an in-depth understanding of the customer's strategic direction, culture and business processes so that you talk the same language.

Remember, Executives and Senior Managers think conceptually and strategically. Ask them provocative questions and seek their input. Ask for technical issues to be explained clearly and concisely. Synthesize large amounts of information; **be concise and get to the point quickly.**

Now that you are armed with some key information about this new type of customer, let's look at some ways to get them involved early and determine who the key stakeholders are that will assist you in arranging a meeting and increasing business.

Sam sat back in his chair and realized that he had been approaching his accounts with entirely the wrong focus. He was intrigued to continue reading, but it was getting late and he needed to prepare for the next day's account calls. He still had this nagging thought that all of this sounded great, but he really didn't believe that he could say anything that an Executive or Senior Manager in any of his accounts would want to hear, especially from a salesperson. But before he left his desk, he wrote down this summary:

KEY TAKEAWAYS:

- Exposure to all levels of an organization is one way to ensure you are aware of the rapid changes that occur and will ensure you have multiple connections to maintain your foothold within the organization.
- Executives and Senior Managers have a greater ability to influence the type and amount of business you gain.
- Executives and Senior Managers are able to provide insight into organizational strategy.
- Key decision-makers can often provide you with connections to others.
- Principles for calling on Executives/Senior Managers:
  - Never, never, never sell in the C-Suite.
  - Leverage your advocates to gain access to more decision-makers and opportunities.
  - Develop an in-depth understanding of the customer's strategic direction, culture and business processes so that you talk the same language.

Chapter 1 Check-in Questions

1. **What has changed that requires salespeople to sell broader and deeper?**
   a. Financial impact of decisions is more important
   b. Number of stakeholders has increased
   c. Decision processes have changed
   d. All of the above

2. **During what timeframe are Executives and Senior Managers most likely to be involved during the decision-making process?**
   a. Early
   b. Middle
   c. A and B
   d. Senior Executives are usually involved consistently throughout the process

3. **Which of the following are Executives and Senior Managers the MOST likely to be involved in during the decision-making process?**
   a. Measuring results
   b. Planning implementation
   c. Establishing objectives
   d. All of the above

4. **Which of the following is likely to be of interest to Executives and Senior Managers?**
   a. Understanding the features of your products or services
   b. Learning about the potential value you can bring to the table
   c. Developing a personal relationship with one of their key suppliers
   d. Learning about how your prices compare with others

- To check your answers, turn to page 121.

CHAPTER 2

Meeting and Communicating with Customers

Sam had a restless night as he kept thinking that he really had a lot more to learn, so after tossing and turning most of the night, he was at his desk in his home office the next morning at 5:45 a.m. With his favorite mug full to the brim with hot coffee, he quickly checked his email. There was a new one from Doug.

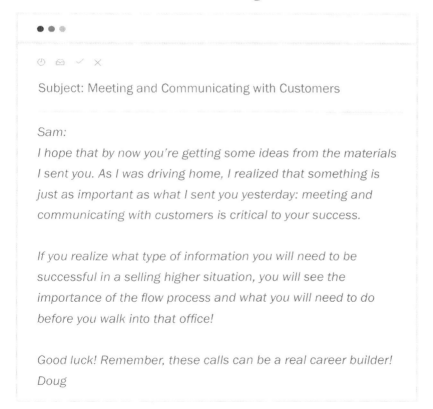

Subject: Meeting and Communicating with Customers

Sam:

I hope that by now you're getting some ideas from the materials I sent you. As I was driving home, I realized that something is just as important as what I sent you yesterday: meeting and communicating with customers is critical to your success.

If you realize what type of information you will need to be successful in a selling higher situation, you will see the importance of the flow process and what you will need to do before you walk into that office!

Good luck! Remember, these calls can be a real career builder!
Doug

Sam took a long sip of coffee as he began reading the attachment that Doug sent him, titled "Meeting and Communicating with Customers."

Here's what he found:

When communicating with Executives and/or Senior Managers, salespeople tend to focus on the specifics of their products and services at the expense of a discussion focused on industry or business-specific initiatives and issues. *This tendency was cited by many Executives and Senior Managers as a common mistake and one that is difficult for salespeople to overcome*.

What can be concluded as most important from the study conducted by Yukon Training and the Business Department at Virginia Tech is that the best way to show Executives/Senior Managers that you deserve to be in their offices is to quickly demonstrate your understanding of the key issues most important to them.

Demonstrate Understanding of Key Issues:
1. Know the business of Executives/Senior Managers (don't waste their time)
2. Focus on and be knowledgeable of key issues that exist for Executives/Senior Managers (talk to them, exchange ideas, don't talk about products right away)
3. Provide ideas or information that will help solve problems and improve outcomes for Executives/Senior Managers (discuss strategy)

We recommend that you keep the above points in mind as we walk you through the next section – Conducting the Meeting.

Conducting the Meeting:

You are now ready to meet with the Executive and/or Senior Manager. This is your time to demonstrate that you have listened to your customer and are on the "same page." It is also your opportunity to demonstrate how you can assist.

Having worked with over 140,000 salespeople, we know that the below steps will deliver results. However, some situations will call for a different order or deleting a step or two. As professional salespeople know, each selling situation is unique, so go into the call prepared and go with the flow!

To ensure your meeting is successful, follow these steps:

Conduct the Meeting	
	Begin the Meeting
	Frame the Situation
	Qualify the Opportunity
	Discuss Ideas Collaboratively
	Clarify Next Steps
	Gain Commitment

YUKON
©2020 Yukon Training, Inc.

Step 1: Begin the Meeting

THIS FIRST STEP IS OFTEN IGNORED AND CAN MEAN THE DIFFERENCE BETWEEN SUCCESS AND FAILURE!

Establish Equal Business Standing (EBS)

Ways you can obtain Equal Business Standing with your customer:

- Dress appropriately. Conservative dress is appropriate here; leave the new fashion statement for another meeting.
- Use a strong voice and a firm handshake.
- Be confident. Remember you have earned the right to be here. You are a knowledgeable, well-informed businessperson who is here to assist the Executive or Senior Manager.
- Demonstrate that you know the customer's business and are focused on and knowledgeable of issues important to the customer. Ensure you have ideas or information that will help solve problems. You normally can't do this until later in the meeting, but be prepared.
- Avoid thanking them for taking their time to meet with you. This would be appropriate at the end of a meeting but greatly reduces your EBS when used up front. This phrase is also overused by salespeople in general and you definitely want to show that you are different. We recommend that you start by saying something like this, "I have really been looking forward to this meeting." This is not trite and is a great deal more positive.

State Meeting Purpose and Review Agenda

Example 1: I have been looking forward to our meeting today. As we discussed on the phone (in the letter, email, etc.), I am interested in your thoughts about what you see happening in the industry and in your organization regarding these important issues (list issues uncovered during research). I would like to share with you some of our thoughts as well, and what we have learned from others in the industry. The purpose of this meeting is to determine your key strategic issues and see if there is alignment with what we have to offer. Our agenda is as follows (provide a copy of the agenda – verbally or in writing). Is there anything additional you'd like to add? We have 30 minutes scheduled for today. How does that sound to you?

Or, another way to say it might be:

Example 2: I have been looking forward to our meeting today. As we discussed on the phone (in the letter, email, etc.) I am interested in your thoughts about what you see happening in the industry and in your organization regarding these important issues (list issues uncovered during research). I would like to share with you some of our thoughts as well, and what we have learned from others in the industry. The purpose of this meeting is to exchange ideas and to see if there are any ways our two companies can better align on common issues. I would like to tell you a little about us; discuss some of the issues that may be affecting both our companies; see if there are ways to better align; and then, if appropriate, talk about any next steps. We planned this meeting for 30 minutes, are we still okay for that timeframe? Great.

No matter how you say it, without being pushy, you are still establishing EBS, talking like an Executive and building credibility. That Executive or Sales Manager quickly realizes that you are not going to waste their time!

The next step of a winning, professional opening is to:

Provide a Capabilities Presentation
This is usually part of the opening of a meeting with a new customer or new contact. It consists of four elements:
- Who you are.
- How you're different (from other suppliers in the industry).
- How you work with customers to help them succeed.
- Relevant examples.

Here is one of the reasons we highly recommend including a capabilities presentation. This is a story that one of our senior colleagues often tells his audiences.

> Back in my corporate executive days, I agreed, as a favor to a colleague, to meet with a financial planner that he knew. On the day of the appointment, the person walked into my office, sat down, and after very little small talk began peppering me with very personal questions: "How much money do you make?" "How much have you saved for retirement?" "How much longer do you plan on working?" And so on. My immediate reaction was: "Who is this person, and why in the world would I share any of this information with him?" I seriously considered asking him to leave but didn't out of respect for my friend. The meeting continued; however, the entire meeting ended up being a waste of time for both of us.
>
> Think how much differently things might have turned out if the person had opened the meeting like this: "I have 22 years in financial planning and have helped hundreds of clients retire early and wealthy. I am currently working with three of your colleagues, and we've put plans together that will allow them to retire five years earlier than they had planned with an additional $4,000 per month in income. Would you be interested in finding out if we can do the same for you?"
>
> Heck, yes, I'm interested in that conversation! I'll tell you everything you need to know about my finances in order to see if I can do what those guys are doing. The opening statement in either of those cases was no more than 60 seconds, but done correctly, a great capabilities presentation earns you the right to ask for the information that you need from the other party. It gives them an incentive to want to share in hopes that you can solve a problem or add value to their situation.

Let's repeat that last thought — **a great capabilities presentation earns you the right to ask for the information that you need from the other party. It gives them an incentive to want to share in hopes that you can solve a problem or add value to their situation.**

This presentation is anywhere from 45 to 90 seconds and presents a differentiating overview of your company that should cause the customer to think, **"That's interesting, I didn't know that."** You briefly paint a picture of your organization as you want the customer to see it, building a foundation for the ideas you will present later.

One of our colleagues related this story of his experience when calling on an Executive at Reader's Digest:

> Ushered into a beautiful wood-paneled boardroom, he was soon met by the one of the top individuals at Reader's Digest. Following our process, he laid out a verbal agenda followed by a short capabilities presentation that was built around our sales expertise, practical sales experience of at least 25 years and the fact that we often worked with the most seasoned and successful salespeople of our clients. The call just got better and better from there, and Reader's Digest became a client. After an incredible workshop involving Reader's Digest's top 20 salespeople in the nation, the Senior Executive even asked our trainers if they would like to work for them! They declined, but during that conversation, they asked the Executive why Yukon Training was selected, as Reader's Digest had considered many top sales training companies as well as very prestigious universities to teach their people. The reply didn't really surprise our trainers but makes our point: the Executive said that we were the only company that talked about why we were different and remembered that we all had "practical sales experience" and hadn't gone through a class so we could teach others! All of that business came from a capability presentation of less than two minutes!

Here's an example of just one of the capabilities presentations we use.

> "My company, Yukon Training, specializes in the development and delivery of customized training programs to companies around the world. We focus on team members who are directly or indirectly involved in business development. We're unlike other training companies, in that each of our programs is highly customized to the special needs of each of our clients, and our facilitators have at least 25 years of practical experience in sales, account management and senior sales management. We work with our customers to help them solve specific problems related to growing and securing business. For example, one of our clients who is heavily involved in contracting was able to utilize our principles to increase their contract renewal rate by 20% over the previous year while increasing profitability."

Sam paused at this point and made a note: Develop a capabilities presentation and work on an agenda. He was glad that he had talked to Doug. This integrated, proven approach was definitely going to help!

Step 2: Frame the Situation

Take the research and information you gained (more on this later, but for now: without knowing something about their issues and the broader influences on their business, YOU will be at a disadvantage. Don't worry, we will talk you through this step later).

Then do the following:
- Discuss the current industry situation
   - From your research, try to bring out some of the issues that you discovered in the industry that might match this

person's issues and also your capabilities. At this point, you should be talking in "industry terms" and about not the client's direct concerns. You are discussing, informing and only beginning to focus in on a few ideas/issues that could spark an interest in this Executive's mind.

- State the issues you have identified as possible "pain points"
  - If you have already identified some of these problem areas, bring them out and see how the Executive views these areas. Maybe the organization already has them under control, or you bringing them up just reminds the Executive that the organization needs to address these issues sooner rather than later!
- Make it a two-way conversation, for example: "We have worked with others in the industry that say X and Y are big issues. What do you see as issues that could affect this industry now or in the future?"

So, after a brief discussion of industry-related topics, you should take the initiative to transition to the next step, which is discovering IF any of the issues that you just discussed or ones that you uncovered in your research are top-of-mind issues for this particular person.

A transitional statement might be: "Thank you for sharing some of those issues/ideas with me. The ones that stick out in my mind and ones that I have heard from others in similar positions to yours are the impact of 5G and concerns about the security of customer information. Any others?"

With that information in hand, now you can try to "peel the onion" so you can explore whether there are existing or perceived issues that you might be able to resolve in unison to help both organizations (yours and theirs)!

We call this step **Step 3: Qualify the Opportunity**

To qualify the opportunity, you need to:

- Determine which issues are the most important by determining how the issues impact their business.
- Prioritize the issues based on potential impact and your current ability to address the issue. Your ability to filter out the non-essential and get to the substantive issues early gives you more credibility.
- Verify interest in taking action on the confirmed issues.
- Determine what they expect to see as results after addressing the issues.
- Discover the timeframes, budget, decision-making process and anything that will affect decision-making.
- Use this opportunity to go broader and deeper into their organization – with their help!

Executives and others have many concerns that do not require action today or in the near future. You need to identify confirmed issues vs. concerns. To do that, you need to put their concerns through the funneling process.

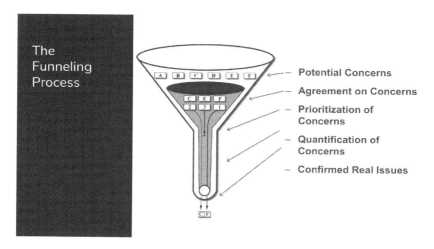

You need to examine potential concerns, agree on concerns, prioritize those concerns and quantify the concerns to determine the confirmed real issues.

To do this effectively you can use the Five I's questioning approach to ensure you are asking the right questions AND asking them at the right time. The funneling process helps you keep the more open questions higher in the funnel and the more specific ones lower.

The purpose is to make sure that you have multiple issues at the top of the funnel so as you select one item and start clarifying with more specific questions, you can determine if that concern is a confirmed real issue or something that can be stopped or put aside easily! It is also critical to have more than one issue at the top of the funnel. Sometimes you may be able to combine several issues into a more complex solution, thus producing a larger win for both organizations!

The five I's consist of questions about:
- Information? – These questions uncover the situation and background of an issue (top of funnel).
- Issue? – These questions uncover the specifics of the issue (top and middle in funnel).
- Impact? – These questions determine the cost of the issue (middle to lower in funnel).
- Intent? – These questions determine what the customer is planning to do about the issue (lower in funnel).
- Improvement? – These questions determine the benefits of addressing the issue (lower in funnel).

Keep in mind these questions are asked in reference to the issues that have been identified and prioritized. By asking the Five I's, you will be able to effectively take your customer's potential concerns and determine their confirmed real issues.

Examples of the Five I's

Information Questions:
(NORMALLY TOP OF FUNNEL QUESTIONS)
- Tell me a little bit about *[the situation, where you find yourself with respect to* _____, *what's going on with* _____, *etc …]*.
- What do you seek to accomplish?
- What are your objectives?
- How will decisions be made about what to do?

Issue Questions:
(TOP OR NEAR THE TOP OF FUNNEL QUESTIONS)
- What specific problems are you hoping to solve?
- Who are the stakeholders? Who is affected by the issues you have raised? What do they think?
- What are the major challenges your organization faces this year?

Impact Questions:
(USE ONCE AN ISSUE IS IDENTIFIED – MID TO LOWER FUNNEL QUESTIONS)
- What measures that you are tracking are being affected?
- How are outcomes being affected?
- How is this issue affecting your institution/department/etc.?
- How does it impact other initiatives that are underway?

Intent Questions:
(LOWER FUNNEL QUESTIONS)
- What are the plans to address this?
- How are you addressing that issue today?
- What types of solutions are you considering, if any?
- Where are you investing your resources for the future? Why?

Improvement Questions:
(LOWER FUNNEL QUESTIONS)
- How will the solutions you are considering address the impacts we discussed earlier?
- What would be the ideal outcomes if this situation were resolved effectively?
- What benefits do you expect to see when the situation is resolved?
- What will it mean to you personally to achieve this success?

How long does it take to take an issue from the top of the funnel to the bottom, determining if you have something to work with? Maybe three to five minutes. So, in a 30-minute call, you most likely have time to explore two to three items. From our experience, we realize that this technique is easy to talk about but really difficult to execute.

The reason why this technique is so difficult should be obvious to many salespeople – we have been trained to listen for those buying signals and when we hear agreement, we REACT! This is not wrong on some calls, but in selling higher, this can result in an abrupt end to something that was going so well. Remember, you are not there to sell anything because EXECUTIVES DON'T BUY! So, the rule to remember is Don't Sell in the Funnel! You are gathering information and clarifying issues.

So, you must resist the temptation to jump on that one idea because your purpose is to find multiple issues and use this opportunity to go broader and deeper into that account. Having multiple issues in your arsenal also gives you a better chance for success in case one of those issues is something that your capabilities and resources cannot address! What's the next step?

NOTE TO READER: At this point you might be asking: Why did I meet with this Executive, who doesn't buy anything?

Great question!

The main reasons that you are there are to:
- Build a relationship.
- Confirm what THEY are trying to accomplish in their business.
- Then have a discussion (below) that would focus on those issues.

You meet with the Executive because you would be willing to meet with others in their organization (remember – broader and deeper) to discover how the others are dealing with those same issues and then COME BACK to this Executive with some ideas that might help them move forward or resolve one or more of the items you discussed.

Congratulations! You have now brought two or three items down the funnel, and you have some ideas as to how your company may help this Executive make some headway with these confirmed real issues that they have said they want to solve.

Step 3: Discuss Ideas Collaboratively

To discuss ideas collaboratively, you need to:

- **Summarize issues** – The best way to summarize is to say something like this "Thank you! This has been a great discussion about some industry issues and how some of these and others might impact your business model. What I heard was that the issue of protecting customer information, especially in the cloud, and getting ready to take advantage of the implementation of 5G networks are especially important to you. Did I get those correct? Are there any others that I missed?"

- **Determine improvements the customer seeks and the impact of any solutions** – Here, you might say something like, "From what we discussed, I had the distinct feeling that you have had some people working on these issues, but they are in the early stages of exploring what options to present to you and others in top management. Am I on track? Good, and we briefly touched on what might happen if either of these initiatives were not in place when competitors took the lead in these areas. We agreed that you want your company to be the innovator!"

- **Share initiatives/strategic direction** – "We have other customers, in non-competing industries, who are working on similar but not exactly the same initiatives, and not only have we been able to help them but we have also benefited from that work. In fact, our CEO had us start on these similar initiatives internally, so at this point, we are way ahead of the learning curve."

- **Test feasibility of your ideas** – CAUTION: You do not want to assume that you can solve their issue(s) after this brief conversation! A good approach might sound like this: "Even though it appears on the surface that we may be able to lend some assistance if you wanted some outside help, I honestly don't know if we would be the right fit, so I do not want to even suggest that at this point. I do believe, though, that we share some common concerns and interests and we both need more information."

- **Confirm sense of urgency** – "Based on our conversation and the fact that you want to be an innovator in these areas, I assume that your timeframe for getting these initiatives implemented is sooner rather than later. Correct?"

Step 4: Clarify Next Steps

To clarify next steps, you need to:
- **Summarize discussion/Agree on next steps –**

Before we give you an example, we want to point out a couple of learning points from experience. First, since this Executive typically doesn't buy anything, this MUST be a "soft close." Second, because they usually like to control meetings/people, give them the chance to make the decision on next steps, but always suggest what you think a good next step might be before giving them their choice!

Okay, here's a sample "next step" close. Use your own style and your own words, but feel free to borrow some of these. "Again, this has been an enlightening conversation. Based on our brief discussion, it appears that we may be able to add value in these areas of data security and implementing 5G networks. What I would like to recommend is that I meet with a few others in your organization and get more insight on how we might be able to help, and then get back with you for a report and see where we go from there. Those are my thoughts. What do YOU see as the next step?"

After speaking with a Chairman/CEO and the COO of a large medical company a few years ago, two of our colleagues shared this story:

The meeting was going great! They had followed what we teach – the opening, the capabilities presentation, the industry situation, a great discussion with questions throughout the funnel and a summary with several problem areas in which they wanted to possibly engage us to help. They knew that the COO was a tough negotiator and handled most of the day-to-day operations, but the Chairman/CEO was much more a strategic thinker and all-around nice guy. So, at the end of the summary, they directed this question to the Chairman/CEO "What do you see as the next step?" He immediately replied, "I want the salesforce to be able to do these 3 critical things we discussed. Let's do it!" And to his COO, "Don't worry about the budget; I want these things implemented quickly!" With that, he got up and left the boardroom! Before the 2 colleagues could even smile, the COO started scolding them for closing the sale! He even said, "I was going to beat you up on the price, but you jumped ahead and got the okay! Then he smiled and said, "That's the way I want my people to handle a call and get the business!"

By the way, our people didn't do a hard close—they simply said, "What do you see as the next step?"

The key here is to use this meeting to BROADEN and DEEPEN your penetration of this account — and with the Senior Manager giving you permission to do so, you are on your way to success!

- **Create a loop back to the Executive/Senior Manager.**
  You worked hard to get the first appointment, so take our advice and DON'T LEAVE THAT OFFICE WITHOUT GETTING THE SECOND APPOINTMENT! It's not difficult to say something like: "With your permission, we will schedule a follow-up meeting in 3 weeks with your assistant. After we meet internally with some of the people you have suggested, we will summarize our findings and report back to you on the possibility of working together on this initiative. Neither of us can say at this point if it's feasible, so we will do some of the legwork and see what's possible."

  The same goes for phone calls. Always try to schedule the next appointment as you are speaking with them.

- **Close the meeting.**
  This is an easy step but critically important to letting this Executive know that you are professional and organized! In your closing statement, state what you will be doing and remind them what they need to do as you start this team effort. We have often said, "This has really been a great meeting. Our next steps will be to:
  1. Work with your assistant to arrange appointments with your people whom you have recommended.
  2. Meet internally with some of our experts to see what resources we might be able to bring to the table.
  3. Following those steps, put a report together with pros and cons and present to you and your team.

  We are looking forward to our next meeting!"

Sam went into the kitchen and grabbed some chips and a bottled water. While opening his bag of chips, he was thinking about what he had just read. His initial reaction was to think: "This could be a lot of work. What initiative could we talk about?" But now he was feeling more confident about how he could make this happen at PATH International. It was all laid out for him; now, he needed to figure out how to execute the plan. He knew that he needed to finish reading, but for now, he was heading out to the backyard to his favorite chair to just relax.

Two hours later, Sam began reading the last part of Chapter 2.

Step 5: Gaining Commitment

After finishing the meetings with the people to whom the Executive has sent you and then working with your internal staff and managers to develop a strategy for possibly working with this customer, the next step is to prepare for the second meeting.

This is much more of an executive-style briefing than a major presentation. We recommend you prepare an executive summary that would contain the following:

A. The problem(s) to be resolved
B. Summary of findings
   1. The issues uncovered through interviews/meetings
   2. Both pros and cons of collaboration between your organization and theirs

3. Possible challenges
4. Possible benefits

C. Recommendations
1. How to start the initiative
2. How your company can help
3. Resources that will be needed by both companies

With the above in hand, the meeting would often flow like this:

- Provide a brief opening.
  - Give a quick overview of what steps were taken to get to now.
- Provide the executive summary of findings/recommendations.
  - Usually presented in a nice binder to everyone present.
- Present a value proposition. (more details on this in Chapter 6)
  - Point out the benefits of moving forward.
  - Point out the anticipated costs/resources required for moving forward.
  - Explain what the costs of not moving forward might mean to both companies.
- Ask for commitment.
  - The next step question works well again here!
- Close the meeting.
  - Summarize the answer to the next step question.
  - Summarize the quick action plan of follow-up.
  - Exit.

Sam was elated. He felt that he could make this happen in due time, but he had more questions about whom to see, how to get the appointment and more. But for now, he decided to write down what he had learned in Chapter 2. Here is what he wrote:

KEY TAKEAWAYS:

- To demonstrate understanding of key issues:
    - Know the Executive/Senior Manager's business (don't waste their time).
    - Focus on and be knowledgeable about issues that exist for the Executive/Senior Manager (talk to them, exchange ideas, don't talk about products right away).
    - Provide ideas or information that will help solve problems and improve outcomes for the Executive/Senior Manager (discuss strategy).
- To ensure your meeting is successful follow these steps:
    - Open the Meeting.
    - Frame the Situation.
    - Qualify the Opportunity.
    - Discuss Ideas Collaboratively.
    - Clarify Next Steps.
    - Gain Commitment.
- Frame the situation by:
    - Discussing the current industry situation.
    - Stating "pain points."
    - Making the conversation two-way.
- Qualify the opportunity by:
    - Determining important issues based on impact on business.
    - Prioritizing issues based on impact and ability to address.
    - Verify interest in taking action on confirmed issues.
    - Using questions like the 5 I's to gain understanding.
- To discuss ideas collaboratively, you need to:
    - Summarize issues.
    - Determine improvements the customer seeks and potential impact of solution.
    - Share initiatives/strategic direction.

- To clarify next steps, you need to:
    - Summarize discussion.
    - Agree on next steps: this is critical to move the process forward.
    - Create a loop back to the Executive/Senior Manager.
    - Close the meeting.
- To gain commitment, there is almost always a separate follow-up meeting with the Executive/Senior Manager. Make sure to do the following:
    - Provide a brief opening.
    - Provide an executive summary of findings/recommendations.
    - Present a value proposition.
    - Ask for commitment.
    - Close the meeting.

Chapter 2 Check-in Questions

1. **Which of the following is the best way to begin an executive meeting?**
   a. Thank the Executive for taking time out of their busy schedule to meet with you
   b. Diffuse any tension by engaging in a short amount of small talk (weather, sports, etc.)
   c. State that the purpose of the meeting is to determine their issues
   d. Tell the Executive how much you admire his/her company

2. **Which of the following is the best way to frame the situation in a meeting?**
   a. List the steps the company has taken in response to challenges
   b. State current industry situations and possible issues for the company
   c. Discuss the company's margins over the past 12 months
   d. Ask about the major strategic initiatives in their company

3. **Which of the following is the main benefit of qualifying the opportunity?**
   a. It allows you the opportunity to discuss your product or service
   b. It communicates to the Executive that your company is selective in picking its clients
   c. It leads you to determine the next best step
   d. It determines which issues are the most important to the Executive/Senior Manager

4. **Which of the following is the purpose of discussing ideas collaboratively with Executives and Senior Managers?**
   a. To persuade them that your solutions match their concerns
   b. To discuss ideas that may be able to address confirmed issues
   c. To point out features and benefits of your services/products relative to their confirmed issues
   d. To show them you are interested in their issues

5. **Which of the following is true of the purpose of the gaining commitment stage of an Executive/Senior Manager meeting?**
   a. To summarize the discussion
   b. To agree on next steps
   c. To set a date and time for the next meeting
   d. To present an executive summary of findings and recommendations

- To check your answers, turn to page 121.

CHAPTER 3

Gaining Access

Sam was busy for the next two days and really had no time to get back to the materials, so when he got home on Friday night, he immediately went to his computer and turned to the next section Doug had sent him: Gaining Access. "This should help me flesh things out," he thought, "I now know how to conduct the call, but that doesn't help at all unless I can actually see the right people." He started to read …

Although you are now ready to meet with members of the senior management, the challenge is getting in to see them. We have already talked about meeting with the Executive or Senior Manager, but before you can have that critical meeting, you must be able to get there! And, as you've learned, getting there early in the decision process is critical.

So, how do we get there? It would not be truthful to say that it is always easy to meet with the right person in every account. Honestly, sometimes it is not possible — and sometimes, it may not be appropriate. With that understood, let's look at some methods for gaining access.

Most Executives and Senior Managers do not see salespeople; they pay others to do that. Therefore, it takes some skills and techniques to gain access. In order to understand practically how best to access Executives and Senior Managers, it is best to hear from them directly. The data below from a study conducted by Yukon Training and the Business Department at Virginia Tech University includes quantitative and qualitative information on what Executives identify as the most effective ways for salespeople to gain access to them.

CHANNELS OF COMMUNICATION

Executive Access

Q. What channels of communication are most effective in gaining access to you?

Rate each channel on a scale from 1 (not effective) to 5 (very effective)

Item	1	2	3	4	5	Mean
Referral from inside source	4	3	11	39	74	4.34
Referral from outside source	7	6	20	76	22	3.76
Email followed by a phone call	19	15	31	53	13	3.20
Direct phone call	25	28	34	27	17	2.87
Written letter followed by phone call	18	35	35	33	10	2.86
Social media groups (LinkedIn, Facebook, Twitter, etc.)	41	19	46	16	9	2.49

When asked what channels of communication were most effective in reaching them, a **majority of Executives indicated that a referral from someone inside their company was most effective**.

Over 86% of the Executives surveyed rated a referral from an inside source as an effective method for gaining access to them, with a full 56% of the total population rating this method as very effective. Executives place great trust and credibility in the recommendations of others inside the organization. This single finding makes the case for building a broad network of relationships inside the client organization as a path toward meeting with Senior Executives inside the company.

Referrals from an outside source were second on their list.

Recommendations from individuals outside the organization also scored high, with 75% of Executives rating that method as effective. The number of individuals rating it as very effective, however, was lower than for internal referrals (17%).

MANAGED MARKETS DATA

Since many of our readers may be involved in the healthcare sector, the study also segmented data from Executives in the Managed Care or Managed Markets. Here is that data, as well:

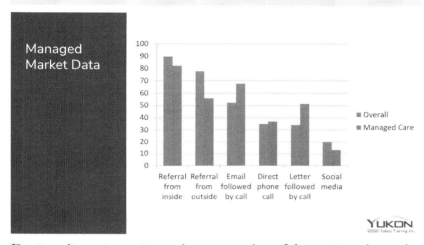

Managed Market Data

YUKON
©2020 Yukon Training, Inc.

During direct interviews, there was a lot of discussion about the method of "cold calling." Much of this discussion was initiated by the Executives without prompting. While the overall mean response was not high (33% rating it as effective), responses to the effectiveness of direct phone calls were fairly evenly distributed across the rating scale. However, the effectiveness of this method as a whole was significantly higher than in previous research.

Jill Konrath, in her book Selling to Big Companies, says that the most success sales professionals who get in to see Executives use a combination of all of the techniques we have discussed. The issue is having a clear and consistent message delivered in various ways. Obviously, if you call an Executive every four or five days for two or three weeks, you will irritate them. So, use phone calls, emails, letters, contacts, administrative assistants, etc. to get your message to the target Executive. It may take multiple methods as well as tries to eventually get to see the correct person! Remember: There is a fine line between persistence and annoyance. Don't cross the line!

DIFFERENTIATING TECHNIQUES

Executive Expectations

Q. Once granted a meeting with you, what is the best way for a salesperson to differentiate himself or herself?

Rate each channel on a scale from 1 (not effective) to 5 (very effective)

Item	1	2	3	4	5	Mean
Responsiveness to your requests and questions	5	2	19	35	70	4.38
Ability to provide accurate comparison of capabilities to goals	6	6	11	45	63	4.17
Thorough understanding of business environments and markets	6	5	16	47	57	4.10
Track record of accomplishments within your industry	4	4	32	56	35	3.57
Professional presentation and material	5	3	30	64	29	3.83
Apparent authority within his/her own company	9	7	32	56	27	3.65
Professional appearance	8	4	41	64	14	3.55

YUKON
©2020 Yukon Training, Inc.

When asked to identify the best way for a salesperson to differentiate himself or herself from others, the two highest ranking responses were:

1. Responsiveness to requests and questions
2. Ability to provide accurate comparison of capabilities to goals

Following up with customers and providing them with information in a timely manner demonstrates that you care about assisting customers with their challenges and issues. It builds trust and credibility and sets you up almost as a "valued consultant" in their eyes and not just another person trying to sell them something. Your ability to provide an accurate comparison of your capabilities to the company's goals demonstrates that you have truly listened to the customer and are willing and able to align your offerings with their needs. If you are not listening to your customers, you will never know their true needs. If you don't know their true needs, you are likely to try to convince them that what you have to offer will meet their needs, whether or not your company can actually deliver; unfortunately, this type of pitch will not "resonate" with them and you will lose the sale and, worse, you will lose credibility.

The next category was "thorough understanding of business environments and markets." As you saw in the previous chapter about conducting the call, of key importance in that call is your ability to discuss "industry and market issues." Executives rank that high on their expectations of your discussion. Being prepared for that type of discussion takes real effort and research, which we will talk about in Chapter 5. But for now, just keep in mind that you will not be able to dodge or bluff your way through these critical discussions. Once you have gained fluency in and deep understanding of these issues, though, you will have established a high degree of credibility!

The other categories in the Executive Expectations chart are important, but notice that they are much less important to most Executives. We have already talked about the need to dress and act professionally. Those should be a given!

Sam was hungry and needed to stop reading, but again, he was gaining confidence that armed with this information, he would be able to put together a plan to get in to those offices at PATH International. He decided to wait until morning to start looking at the other access techniques. Before he left his computer, though, he sent a quick message to Doug.

Subject: Thanks for the help!

Doug, Sam here. I am learning a lot from the materials you sent me. Just a note to say thanks for the help! Dinner is on me the next time we get together!

Sam

On Saturday morning, Sam was back at his computer. He began reading the other access techniques. Here is what he discovered about contacting Executives and Senior Managers initially to get an appointment:

Communicating with Executives and Senior Managers differs from other interactions in that most "small talk" items should be minimized. If you choose one of the direct approaches (more on this later) — phone call, email or letter followed by a phone call — one of the following should occur:

- Executive/Senior Manager answers the call directly.
- You get his or her voice mail.
- The Administrative Assistant answers.
- Your email or letter is screened by the Administrative Assistant then passed on to the Executive/Senior Manager.
- As a gatekeeper, the Administrative Assistant screens your email or letter and discards it.

There's a funny story that one of our workshop attendees told about a salesperson who called a C-Suite office at 6:45 a.m. to leave a message about setting up an appointment. As he called the number, he had his script in hand and was ready to leave a message.

To his shock, the Executive picked up the phone and said, "Hello." The salesperson, a little startled, stumbled on his words: "Oh, I didn't think you would be there this early in the morning!"

The Executive responded, "Then why did you call?"

The salesperson never really recovered from that exchange, and needless to say, this Executive is still on the "no see" list.

We recommend that when you make a call to a customer, you always plan for the possible scenarios:
- The person will answer.
- You will have to leave a message on voicemail.
- You will speak to the person's assistant and leave a message.

Always plan for all three.

You need to prepare for each level of screening.

No matter which of the above occurs, keep the following in mind:
- State only two to three issues.
  - Based on your research, determine the top-of-mind issues to the Executive/Senior Manager and the industry.
  - If you are creating an email or letter, make sure to use bullets. This keeps the Executive/Senior Manager or Administrative Assistant from having to dig through a paragraph to find the key points. Without bullets, they won't read the email; it will be deleted.
- Discuss the fact that your company sees these issues as

important, too, and that you have worked with other companies to address these issues with success.

- Imply that you don't know how important these issues are to the Executive/Senior Manager, but ask for an opportunity to meet face-to-face to share ideas on how to deal with them.
- Don't try to sell over the phone.
- Provide a target market "elevator speech*" of one to two sentences:
  - Who you work with (target market).
  - How you help your customers.
  - What makes your company unique.
- Close by saying that the meeting will take about 30 minutes and that you will call the office on a specific date to arrange a convenient time to meet.

---

*SEE APPENDIX II FOR ELEVATOR SPEECH EXAMPLES

Executive Outreach

Executive:

While talking with our partners and customers in the healthcare industry, we have found that many are concerned about:

- Managing the high cost of care related to certain disease states
- Controlling the costs associated with length of stay issues
- The impact of healthcare reform on standards of care, reimbursement. and long-term sustainability

Finding creative solutions, we believe, is critical to the success of everyone involved in healthcare.

If any of these issues are a challenge to you and your organization, I would welcome the opportunity to learn more about your unique situation, share some of the things we have learned from other healthcare executives, and jointly determine if and how we might be able to help.

I will call your office on next Wednesday, at 9:00 am to arrange a convenient time to meet.

Ron

Ron Lambert
Director of National Accounts
555-555-5555

Keep in mind that the way to treat the Administrative Assistant is the same way you would treat the Executive. The Administrative Assistant will almost always control access to the Executive, be aware of the strategic issues, and appreciate you treating him/her as part of the executive team.

OTHER GAINING ACCESS STRATEGIES

1. Ask your regular contact questions they *cannot* answer.

Example: "Our company is trying to match long-range plans with our key customers' goals. What are the top three or four strategic goals from the perspective of your strategic decision-makers?"

Asking these types of questions allows you to sell the advantage of meeting with Executives and Senior Managers. Think about this: How often do you suppose your contact gets to meet with the top-tier Executives in their company? In most companies, not often or never! If appropriate, you can even suggest that your contact be in that future meeting as well! Let them know that you can share ideas with their Executives and Senior Managers, as well as how your company has developed or is developing capabilities that can possibly help them achieve their strategic goals. To make yourself even more credible, bring a Senior Manager from your company or a subject matter/industry expert.

2. Create value, and use that to gain higher access

We all talk about adding value to our products and services, but sometimes we might forget that value is really about what the customer believes is valuable to them. With that in mind, think about someone who might be inside a prospect organization or an account who might really be trying to show THEIR value to people inside their organization. If you can provide that for them, you may have just created a true advocate! One of our colleagues, Alyssa, had been trying to get into an account for quite a while with absolutely no success at any level. She decided to provide value first at a lower level to see if that would finally create that "toehold." So, she invited analyst-level people to an event that would be beneficial to them. One responded but had a conflict for that day. Our colleague offered to take good notes and give the analyst a call after the event to share the takeaways. Following the event, Alyssa called, and they had a stimulating conversation about the subjects at the event. In that call, after sharing her notes, Alyssa learned more about the account and the technology the company was currently using. Fast forward a few weeks, and there was another event in the area. Alyssa invited that same individual and offered to stop by her office before the event to meet in person. The analyst not only agreed but asked if this could be more of a formal meeting, as she wanted to include her boss – the person Alyssa had been trying to see from the beginning!

Adding value here created the opportunity to move higher.

3. Ask an advocate to arrange a meeting

While meeting with a person in your account who is not only your advocate but also has ideas on how their company and yours might work together, suggest that they invite some of his company's Executives to a joint meeting. This will assist the advocate with his ideas and get you in front of those you are trying to meet. During the meeting, promote your advocate's ideas while discussing strategy and your capabilities with the Executives and/or Senior Managers.

4. Work within organizations, clubs and industry associations

Joining industry associations and participating actively will allow you to socialize with Executives and Senior Managers at a neutral site designed for interaction among members. A friend of one of our senior people has been highly successful in the construction industry by joining multiple state and regional construction associations AND being active enough to be selected to some associations' boards of directors and numerous industry committees. Great idea!

5. Speak to their organization or at a conference sponsored by the organization

Somewhat related to the idea above, become an expert speaker in a subject of interest to the Senior Manager at an organization/department meeting or to an association/club to which they belong. Doing this shows Executives and Senior Managers that you are more than a supplier — you are an information resource.

6. Sponsor executive focus groups

Work with your advocate to invite Executives and/or Senior Managers to participate in focus groups on issues important to the industry. Invite Executives and/or Senior Managers from other non-competing organizations. This provides them with strategic industry information, gives them an opportunity to network with peers, affords them recognition as an "outside expert" and demonstrates that you are a resource for information and contacts. Provide a plaque or some other recognition for their participation. One of our colleagues used this method repeatedly to reach key Executives who were "unreachable" otherwise!

7. Conduct a company tour

If appropriate, have your advocate arrange an opportunity for you to invite Executives and/or Senior Managers to come to your workplace for a tour. Follow up the tour with a business or industry review. Again, if appropriate, top off the day with a lunch/dinner or some entertainment. This gets the Executives and/or Senior Managers out of their environment and into yours, allowing for more focused interactions.

8. Use social media

Although social media did not rank as high as other gaining access techniques in our study, the use and acceptability of these tools have increased. Sites such as LinkedIn have become mainstream and allow business professionals to connect with one another via the internet. Social media are vast and ever growing, so staying up to date on the opportunities social media present can assist you in your ability to gain access.

You should be LinkedIn to all of your customers – it's a great way to see what they highlight about themselves and can give you some valuable insights.

You should also set up Google alerts for your key customers and accounts, to be notified of any news that becomes available about them.

Sam wrote in his notebook some of the things he had just read.

KEY TAKEAWAYS:

- A referral from someone inside the company was most effective at gaining access.
- Use a variety of communication methods (phone, emails, letters, admin, etc.) to get your message to the target.
- Best way for salespeople to differentiate themselves:
  - Responsiveness to requests and questions.
  - Ability to provide accurate comparison of capabilities to goals.
- Gaining access strategies:
  - Ask your customer questions they cannot answer.
  - Ask an advocate to arrange a meeting.
  - Work within organizations, clubs and industry associations.
  - Use social media.

Chapter 3 Check-in Questions

1. **Which of the following channels of communication is most effective in reaching Executives and Senior Managers?**
   a. A direct phone call
   b. A written letter
   c. A referral from inside their company
   d. Social media

2. **Which of the following techniques is most effective in differentiating yourself?**
   a. Responsiveness to requests and questions
   b. Professional appearance
   c. Track record of accomplishments
   d. Ability to make the customer comfortable

3. **Why is asking your contact a question they can't answer an effective gaining access strategy?**
   a. Demonstrates your knowledge expertise
   b. Reinforces the company's need to hire you
   c. Enables you to see how much power your contact has
   d. Allows you to sell the advantage of meeting with Executives and Senior Managers

4. **How would speaking at a conference sponsored by the Executive/Senior Manager's organization help you gain access?**
   a. It allows them to see you in action
   b. It shows them that you are a potential source of information
   c. You will have a chance to meet them after the presentation
   d. Since they are interested in your topic, they will be more likely to want to meet with you.

- *To check your answers, turn to page 121.*

CHAPTER 4

Engaging Your Customers

Sam needed to stop, as he had to do some shopping and get other things done. He decided that before he stopped for the day, he would read his notes from each chapter. "That way," he thought, "as I'm doing some other things today, I can start putting some ideas together for PATH International." He felt good as he left his house 20 minutes later. It was going to be a great day!

The next day, Sam had set his alarm to get up early, and at 6:30 a.m., he was greeted by his favorite Queen song, "We Are the Champions." After a quick shower and a hearty breakfast of eggs and bacon, he sat down at his desk with his cup of strong black coffee. Today was the day he needed to make some headway into the next chapter of information Doug had sent. It looked interesting, but challenging. He started to read…

As we have already mentioned several times, the key to getting Executives and Senior Managers involved early in the process is to demonstrate that you understand their business. This is not a new concept; we all know we need to understand our customers' business. However, knowing who they are and what they do is not enough! To really impress your customers, you need to dig deep.

Before you think it, let us say it: Many salespeople, not you of course, want to completely skip over these steps and get right to the meeting.

CAUTION: UNLESS YOU ARE LUCKY, GETTING IN FRONT OF A KEY EXECUTIVE AND/OR A SENIOR MANAGER WITHOUT TRULY UNDERSTANDING THEIR BUSINESS COULD AND MOST LIKELY WILL RESULT IN YOU NEVER ACHIEVING A CALL HIGHER IN THE ORGANIZATION AGAIN AND COULD ALSO POSSIBLY HURT YOUR EFFORTS THROUGHOUT THE ENTIRE ACCOUNT!

So, please, take the time to learn more about what they are thinking and doing on a daily basis before initiating that meeting.

Following these four steps will ensure you conduct research on the areas that will assist you in engaging your customers in a broader and deeper manner.

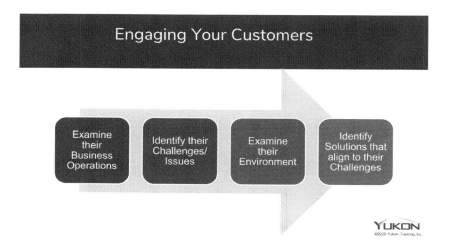

Step 1.

Examine their Business Operations. How do they make money? What are they accountable for? What is their business model? Being knowledgeable in this space will build credibility.

Step 2.

Identify their Challenges/Issues. Have an understanding of what their top-of-mind challenges/issues are and how they might relate to your company's capabilities.

Step 3.

Examine their Environment. What do they value? Who influences whom? What terminology do they use? Understanding the organizational and department culture and how they prefer to interact will assist you in broadening and deepening your connections.

Step 4.

Identify Solutions that align to their Challenges. Determine what you have to offer that will provide solutions to their challenges.

To tackle these steps successfully **you have to conduct some research**. This will take time, but it will be time well invested. We are going to give you some important pointers so you can make this activity more efficient and less time consuming.

1. Examine their Business Operations

To gain a deeper understanding of your customer's business operations you will need to look at a variety of information.

Determine Sources of Information

To begin, think about what sources of information you will use to gain insight into your customer's business. Since we are living in the digital age, most research can be done online.

Think about a current customer you work with or a new customer you would like to have. What information would tell you the most about their business? The most obvious choice is the company website. This was probably your first choice, and it's a good one.

Company Website
There is normally a lot of information on a company's website, including:
- An online version of the shareholder annual report.
- Insight into strategic direction.
- Presentations.
- Information on business, markets and services.
- Recent news postings and press releases.
- Biographies of Executives.
- Employee newsletters.
- Organization Charts.

Some of these are straightforward and need no further explanation, so we are just going to point out the KEYS to open the door for you. If they are a publicly traded company, you will find more information. WHY? Publicly traded companies are required by the U.S. Securities and Exchange Commission (SEC) to report certain information to shareholders and those who might want to become shareholders. There is less information available for privately owned companies, and we will address that later on in this section.

A CLOSER LOOK AT THE SHAREHOLDER ANNUAL REPORT

This report contains the following:
- Letter to the Shareholders
- Additional Narrative Section
- Financial Information
- Management's Discussion and Analysis of Results
- Officers and Directors

The Letter to the Shareholders provides information about the strategic direction of the company, significant accomplishments of the previous year and future plans and initiatives. THIS IS A MUST-READ for all of us in sales. A quick example will help you understand why it is so important.

> One of our colleagues was working with an account team that wanted to penetrate much higher levels of one of the largest chemical companies. The first assignment our colleague gave the account team was to read the Letter to the Shareholders written by the chemical company's Chairman of the Board. This was a typical letter that normally is no longer than two pages. After the account team read the Chairman's letter, our colleague asked this question, "Who can tell me how this Chairman will be compensated this coming year?" After a few incorrect guesses, our colleague said, "Count the number of times that the letter mentions ROI (return on Investment)!" A fast reader called out, "17 times." Yes, 17 times in a short page-and-a-half letter! No doubt what was on the mind of the Chairman! And you can image, every senior officer and department head in this company was aware that the goal that year was to increase ROI! From our experience, we can tell you that probably few people calling on this company that year understood that management driver, and most probably tried to sell their products or services just like anyone else. Instead, they should have been developing a plan on HOW their product or service could have helped the company increase its ROI.

The next section, the Additional Narrative Section, is probably the least useful to most of us in sales, but it's still worth a quick glance as it contains narrative sections that describe various things including business units, company initiatives, current and new markets, and community and charitable interests. This section is usually printed on glossy paper with plenty of pictures of employees in their involvement in the organization and in the wider community.

If the company is publicly traded, the Financial Information section includes income statements, balance sheets and more in-depth numbers that we will discuss shortly. Management Discussion and Analysis of Results usually has no pictures and is in a smaller font. This is a section **they do not want you to read**. But it is the section **you should read** since it is here that you are most likely to find the "pain" the organization is facing. These are areas that will be top-of-mind to an Executive and could be your pathway to a meeting with Executives and Senior Managers. Always look at the list of Officers and Directors, since there may be connections between your company and the organization/department of which you were unaware. Also, there may be connections with other customers.

Industry Sites

It's also important to understand the company's industry. Reading industry publications, articles and even blogs can provide you with information that can expose internal and external challenges Executives may be facing. Being able to refer to some of these articles can certainly impress an Executive. For key customers, sign up online for daily emails and business alerts, and have the information come to you.

The News

Don't forget to check the news! Logging into these various sites and typing in the company name can provide you with a ton of valuable information.

- Nexus.com
- Business Week
- Wall Street Journal
- Google Alerts

Targeted Searches and Making Connections

If you know the name of the Executive you'd like to meet, do a search online and see if you can find any quotes from speeches or articles featuring the Executive. Referring to an article or presentation by the Executive will undoubtedly increase your credibility and improve your relationship with the Executive. Again, use LinkedIn to connect with all of your customers and prospects.

Financial Sites

If you really want to know about your customer's business and the challenges/issues they face, start looking at their company's financial information. Here are two websites that provide financial information:

- D&B Hoovers™ (Hoovers.com). This website allows you access to financial information and strategy, and it even identifies the company's competition. Some information is free, and you can subscribe to get even more information.
- Barrons.com. This website provides in-depth analysis and commentary on the markets, updated every business day online. This is a great source for business news, and it offers subscription options for more in-depth information.

Financial information can also be found in the annual report. There are two types of annual reports. The shareholder annual report is the glossy document a company sends to its shareholders when it holds an annual meeting to elect directors. The 10-K annual report must be submitted to the SEC annually. Keep in mind that some companies combine the annual report and the 10-K into one document. Typically, the 10-K contains much more detail than the annual report. It includes information such as company history, organizational structure, executive compensation, equity, subsidiaries and audited financial statements, among other information.

You can find a company's 10-K report by going to:
www.sec.gov/edgar/searchedgar/companysearch.html.

If your customers are not publicly held companies, try to acquire as much information as possible on everything except the detailed financial information, since that is often not readily available. All information you collect needs to be categorized and checked for accuracy (consider the source). Be sure to double check your information for verification.

2. Identify their Challenges/Issues

Now that you have examined a substantial amount of information on your customer, you need to know how to interpret it to identify their challenges/issues. One of the best ways to do this is to conduct a financial analysis.

Conducting a Financial Analysis

Conducting a financial analysis on a company will help you determine:

- Trends in revenue and profitability growth.
- Your customer's gross margin.
- The key drivers that represent your customer's financials and

business model.

When talking with a decision-maker, do you have a clear idea of how their needs affect the cost structure of the company?

Trends in revenue and profitability growth
It is important to look for trends in performance. For example, if the cost of goods sold has been rising faster than revenue over the past three years, there may be a problem on the cost side of the business. There may be a good reason for the increase, but the trend should raise a red flag and cause you to investigate further.

Questions to ask yourself in your research:
- Where do your customers spend money?
- Are these expenditures increasing faster than revenue? If so, can you identify whether the spending is strategic or problematic?
- What impact do these expenditures have on the various levels of profitability?

Your customer's gross margin:
- Is the trend going in the right direction? How does the margin compare to industry standards?

Key drivers that represent your customer's financials and business model:
- Is it Return on Investment?
- Return on Assets?
- Some other measurement?

Ultimately, the answers to the above questions will help you focus on where and how your resources can bring value to your customer.

We mentioned earlier that the financial section of an annual report includes an income statement and a balance sheet. Let's look closely at each one, as they are the sources you will use to answer the questions we have posed above.

Income Statement

An income statement shows how much money a corporation makes or loses. An income statement may also be called a "statement of earnings," an "earnings report," or a "profit and loss report." The income statement is a summary of the results of business activities for a specified period, such as a month or a year. The key elements of the income statement are revenue and expense.

The following are the consolidated statement of earnings and the balance sheet of Home Depot, Inc and Subsidiaries.

THE HOME DEPOT, INC. AND SUBSIDIARIES
CONSOLIDATED STATEMENTS OF EARNINGS

	Fiscal Year Ended[1]		
amounts in millions, except per share data	February 3, 2013	January 29, 2012	January 30, 2011
NET SALES	$ 66,182	$ 71,290	$ 77,357
Cost of Sales	43,754	47,285	51,335
GROSS PROFIT	22,428	24,005	26,022
Operating Expenses:			
Selling, General and Administrative	15,896	17,841	17,038
Depreciation and Amortization	1,692	1,779	1,684
Total Operating Expenses	17,588	19,620	18,722
OPERATING INCOME	4,840	4,385	7,300
Interest and Other (income) Expense:			
Interest and Investment Income	(27)	(27)	(91)
Interest Expense	667	621	694
Other	162	162	—
Interest and Other, net	802	756	603
EARNINGS BEFORE PROVISION FOR INCOME TAXES	4,038	3,629	6,697
Provision for income Taxes	1,357	1,268	2,410
NET EARNINGS	$ 2,681	$ 2,361	$ 4,287
Weighted Average Common Shares	1,589	1,652	1,738
BASIC EARNINGS PER SHARE	$ 1.69	$ 1.62	$ 2.47
Diluted Weighted Average Common Shares	1,601	1,660	1,599
DILUTED EARNINGS PER SHARE	$ 1.67	$ 1.42	$ 2.68

[1] Fiscal year ended February 3, 2013 includes 53 weeks. Fiscal years ended January 29, 2012 and January 30, 2011 include 52 weeks.

Generally, the most important source of income is revenue from the sales of goods and services, called sales or operating revenues. The net sales or net revenue figure typically shown in income statements is the amount received after taking into consideration returned goods and allowing for reduced prices. Companies may also have income from investments, such as interest or dividends. All sources of income are totaled to produce the total revenue figure.

An important financial number to many companies is…

Net Income Before Tax:
When operating expenses and costs are subtracted from the gross revenue figure, the result is called net income before taxes or operating income.

Net Income Before Taxes = Revenue - [Costs + Expenses].

The Balance Sheet
A balance sheet is a statement of the assets, the liabilities and the owner's equity (also called net worth) of a business. As you can imagine, a company's assets and liabilities are continually changing, **so a balance sheet offers a snapshot of the company's financial health at a given point in time**. A balance sheet is a summary of a company's net worth as of a given date.

Balance Sheet
For the Year End 2001 through 2005
(all numbers in 000s)

ASSETS	2001	2002	2003	2004	2005
Current Assets					
Cash and Equivalents	$32,615	$20,576	$295,794	$261,237	$432,893
Net accounts receivable	563,995	361,644	376,110	391,154	469,385
Inventory	500,148	470,693	485,400	500,654	574,162
Other current assets	10,000	10,000	10,000	10,000	10,000
Total Current Assets	**$1,106,758**	**$862,913**	**$1,167,304**	**$1,163,046**	**$1,486,440**
Fixed Assets					
Capital assets	$100,000	$600,000	$600,000	$1,100,000	$1,600,000
Accumulated depreciation	84,000	172,200	264,810	362,051	464,153
Total Net Fixed Assets	**$16,000**	**$427,800**	**$335,190**	**$737,950**	**$1,135,847**
TOTAL ASSETS	**$1,122,758**	**$1,290,713**	**$1,502,494**	**$1,900,995**	**$2,622,287**
LIABILITIES					
Current Liabilities					
Accounts payable	$263,520	$224,895	$233,712	$242,896	$280,910
Short-term notes	70,000	0	0	0	0
Other short-term liabilities	0	0	0	0	0
Total Current Liabilities	**$333,520**	**$224,895**	**$233,712**	**$242,896**	**$280,910**
Long-term liabilities	$225,000	$195,000	$45,000	$45,000	$45,000
Total Liabilities	**$558,520**	**$419,895**	**$278,712**	**$287,896**	**$325,910**
Shareholders' Equity					
Capital stock	$110,000	$110,000	$110,000	$110,000	$110,000
Retained earnings	444,238	750,818	1,103,782	1,493,099	2,176,377
Total Shareholders' Equity	**$554,238**	**$860,818**	**$1,213,782**	**$1,603,099**	**$2,286,377**
TOTAL LIABILITIES & EQUITY	**$1,112,758**	**$1,280,713**	**$1,492,494**	**$1,890,995**	**$2,612,287**

A balance sheet often shows the assets (resources owned by a company) on the left side of the page, and the liabilities (claims against assets or debts owed) and owners' equity (assets minus liabilities) on the right side of the page. The totals on the two sides of the page must be equal. That is why it's called a "balance" sheet. In the example above, the liabilities are listed below the assets.

There are three ways to quickly analyze the many parts of the income statement and balance sheet:
A. Common Size Analysis
B. Percent Change Analysis
C. Key Ratio Analysis

A. Common Size Analysis
Common size analysis converts all the dollar figures on a financial statement into percentages. The percentages then allow you to make more accurate comparisons in your analysis. You can then compare calculations against:

- Previous year
- Industry averages
- Key competitors
- Company targets

Example A: On an income statement, all items might be expressed as a percentage of net sales.

Research expense = $420 million
Net sales = $5,284 million.

Thus, research expense represents 7.9% of net sales revenue. 7.9% may then be compared to:
- Company's prior performance records.
- Industry averages.
- Competitors performance.

Example B: On a balance sheet, all line items might be expressed as a percentage of total assets.

Current assets = $2,294 million
Total assets = $2,744 million

Thus, current assets represent 83.6% of total assets. 83.6% might be compared to:
- Previous years' performance.
- Industry average.
- Competitors performance.

B. Percent Change Analysis

Next, we will look at percent change analysis. Percent change analysis allows you to track changes in financial statements from one reporting period to the next. This approach to analyzing the balance sheet and income statement will be particularly useful in identifying key problem areas in a company. You are then able to compare against:

- Industry averages
- Previous years
- Key competitors
- Company targets
- Inflation

Percentages are calculated by using the following formula:
% Change = [this year's total - last year's total]/last year's

Example A: On an income statement

Net sales for 2020: $5,284 million
Net sales for 2019: $4,017 million

Thus, the percent change in net sales was $1,267 million or 31.5%.

Example B: On a balance sheet

Total assets for 2020 were $454 million
Total assets for 2019 were $400 million

Thus, the percent of change in total assets was $54 million or 13.5%.

C. Key Ratio Analysis

There are three types of key ratio analyses:

- Return on Assets.
- Return on Equity.
- Earnings per Share.

Return on Assets (ROA)

ROA is a measure of the efficiency with which management has invested company assets. This ratio measures the relationship between profitability and investments and draws its data from the balance sheet and the income statement.

Return on Assets = Net Profit (After Taxes)/Total Assets

Return on Equity (ROE)

ROE is a measure of how hard the owner's equity is working.

Return on Equity = Net Income (or Net Profit)/Owner's Equity

Earnings Per Share

Earnings per share is a way of measuring the return to the stockholder. A positive trend (increasing earnings) is a general indicator of the desirability of the stock. Only shares of common stock are used in this calculation.

Example: Suppose that you are getting ready to call on an Executive in Company XYZ and you used the Percentage Change Formula on net sales.

% Change = [this year's total - last year's total]/last year's total

On the income statement, you found the following:
Net sales for 2020: $5,284 million
Net sales for 2019: $4,017 million
Net sales for 2018: $2,852 million

Thus, the percent change in net sales for 2019 to 2020 was $1,267 million or 31.5%. And the percent change from 2018 to 2019 was $1,165 or 40.8%.

As one can see, even though the raw numbers made it look like it was a record increase from 2019 to 2020, actually it was a significant decrease (over 10%) from the year before. So, what does that tell you about the company? At this point you don't know, but it tells you that SOMETHING happened to the net sales increase this year. Now, you need to dig deeper to see if it was an acquisition the year before, or a new product, or that the net sales increase per year might be shrinking. Let's say that you discover that the net sales are decreasing. The next step would be to work on how your products/services might be able to help your customer with increasing their net sales! Now, you have something to possibly explore on your call. Fortunately for you, there aren't too many competitors who are even thinking about what you just learned!

3. Examine their Environment

What do they value? Who influences whom? What terminology do they use?

Understanding the organizational and department culture and how they prefer to interact will assist you in broadening and deepening your connections.

One of the best ways to do this is through networking. Think of networking as creating another salesforce: another group of people who know enough about you and your company to be able to recommend you with confidence to their best customers and friends.

Although there is an abundance of information online about your customers, remember that networking and talking with contacts inside and outside of the organization/department can still be one of the most valuable sources of information that can be found anywhere.

Networking with others can provide you with the following:
- Information on organization/department culture.
  - How closely do they follow process and procedure?
  - Who within the organization/department is the gatekeeper?
  - Who holds the real decision-making power?
  - How do they interact with one another? Who in the organization/department is able to influence decision-makers?
- A person's preference for communication: email, voicemail, lunch requests, etc.
- Past work history and personal interests of personnel to assist in making connections.

4. Identify Solutions that Align to their Challenges

You have done enough research at this point to begin to identify potential solutions that will align with the challenges you uncovered for your customer. Although you have not had an opportunity to discuss the identified challenges with the customer, ensuring that you are able to provide ideas, strategies and tactics to overcome them will assist you when you do have the chance.

To assist you in this exercise, simply create a two-column table in which column one is titled "Customer Challenges" and column two is titled "Possible Solutions."

Customer Challenges	Possible Solutions
% of net sales decreasing	Add new products
	Cull current products
	New markets that you are dominant in

When completing this table, keep in mind that possible solutions are not just your products and services but strategies and/or tactics other companies have used to overcome the challenge. Providing such information to a potential customer can help them trust you and assist in them seeing you as more than just a vendor that provides products and services; it can help the customer see you as a trusted advisor to their business.

Sam just realized that he had been sitting at his desk since early morning and it was now close to 11 a.m. "Thank goodness," he thought, "for the extra day off this week." Before he got up from his desk and started on some projects around the house, he wrote down the following learning points in his notebook, which was rapidly filling up:

KEY TAKEAWAYS:

- The key to getting Executives and Senior Managers involved early in the process is to demonstrate that you understand their business.
- To understand your customer's business, you must engage them by:
  - Examining their business operations.
  - Identifying their challenges/issues.
  - Examining their environment.
  - Identifying solutions that align to their challenges.
- Examine their business operations to determine:
  - How they make money.
  - What they are held accountable for.
  - What their business model is.
- Use multiple sources of information to determine how your customer's business operates.

  To identify your customer's challenges/issues, conduct a financial analysis to determine: Trends in revenue and profitability growth, the key drivers that represent your customer's financials and business model, the income statement and balance sheet.

- There are three ways to analyze the many parts of the income statement and balance sheet:
  - Common Size Analysis.
  - Percent Change Analysis.
  - Key Ratio Analysis.
- Examine your customer's environment to determine:
  - What they value.
  - Who influences whom.
  - What terminology they use.
- Networking with others can provide you with information on organization/department culture, a person's preference regarding communication, past work history and personal interests.

Chapter 4 Check-in Questions

1. **Which of the following is a benefit of conducting research on an Executive/Senior Manager's business operations?**
   a. Understanding their business
   b. Identifying their challenges/issues
   c. Understanding their environment
   d. All of the above

2. **Which of the following provides the most detailed information regarding a company's business?**
   a. The 10-K report
   b. The annual report
   c. Financial publications such as Barron's or barrons.com
   d. Your stockbroker

3. **Which of the following is the best way to identify a company's challenges/issues?**
   a. Ask another company in the industry
   b. Read the Letter to the Shareholders
   c. Conduct a financial analysis
   d. Examine industry blogs

4. **Which of the following is a way to analyze the income statement and balance sheet?**
   a. Key ratio analysis
   b. Common size analysis
   c. Percent change analysis
   d. All of the above

5. **Which of the following is the best way to understand your customer's environment?**

a. Examine the customer's balance sheet
b. Network
c. Read the Letter to the Shareholders
d. Conduct a financial analysis

- To check your answers, turn to page 121.

CHAPTER 5

Broadening and Deepening Your Account Position

While mowing his grass, Sam thought about some additional questions about Chapter 4, so when he finished, he sat back down at his computer and sent an email to Doug.

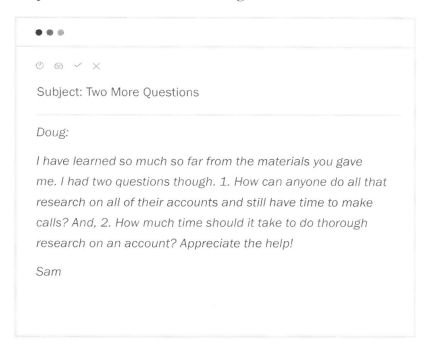

Subject: Two More Questions

Doug:

I have learned so much so far from the materials you gave me. I had two questions though. 1. How can anyone do all that research on all of their accounts and still have time to make calls? And, 2. How much time should it take to do thorough research on an account? Appreciate the help!

Sam

Sam opened his email after dinner that same night. There was an email from Doug.

Re: Two More Questions

Sam:

Good to hear from you! Been out all day with the family and just read your note. Good questions! While some research on all accounts is needed, including current ones, you should save the major research for accounts that you believe are strategic to your total business and others where you must go higher in the organization to go wider and deeper. Your second question is more difficult to answer, but finding and then analyzing a major account could take 3-5 hours spread out over time. Not bad, though, when you look at the potential reward! I'm so glad that you are still learning from the materials. Remember that I used this same material to be Salesperson of the Year in my company!

Doug

So far, we have examined selling higher in this book, and it is important to know that many of the techniques and skills discussed are just as effective when you are trying to broaden and deepen your account position. However, there is one technique — creating an influence map — that will increase your ability to broaden, deepen and strengthen your relationships throughout the organization/department. When you implement this effectively, you are more likely to compete based on the business value you add rather than on price. Also, being well positioned at key levels in the organization/department improves your likelihood of meeting with important Executives and Senior Managers and gaining their support.

To create such a map, you will want to complete the following steps:

1. Examine your business objective for the organization/department.
2. Identify the decision(s) that lead to this objective being accomplished and the key decision-maker who makes them.
3. Map all the people who influence the key decision-maker on EACH decision and their role in the decision-making process.

Example:

Account Business Objective(s):

Objective 1: Gain access to John Smith (Executive) at XYZ account

Decision 1: John Smith needs to agree to meet with me.

Who influences John Smith in decision making of this kind? Erin Cabot (admin), Mike Ramirez (colleague), Dan Bosch influences Mike Ramirez.

Objective 2: Provide information to John Smith regarding ways product X will save XYZ company money.

Let's look at the second part of step three.

3. Map all the people who influence the decision-maker on EACH decision *and* **their role in the decision-making process**

There are seven decision process roles that can exist. As we go through each one, think about the people you have identified as influencers to your key decision-maker and determine which decision role each one plays.

1. Executive Approver
2. Decision-Maker

3. Trusted Advisor
4. Specialist
5. Utilizer
6. Gatekeeper
7. Advocate

It's important to know that:
- The roles are often played by different people for different objectives you have within the same organization/department.
- Some roles may be played by more than one person.
- People's responsibilities may change during the decision process.
- Roles are often played by a committee or an informal group rather than by an individual.
- Roles may not always be "visible."

1. Executive Approver

Role:
- Makes policy decisions and high-level business management decisions
- Rarely ever buys anything

Potential Drivers:
- Profits, growth, strategy
- Policy, organizational progress, vision for the future

Attributes:
- High-level manager with both veto and approval power

Your Goals:
- Identify key Executive Approvers
- Discover their concerns, goals and vision

2. Decision-Maker

Role:
- Gives final approval to buy
- Releases money to buy

Potential Drivers:
- Price performance
- Return on investment

Attributes:
- Tends to be higher in organization as dollar amount of the sale rises
- Tends to be higher in organization in difficult times
- Tends to be higher in organization for new or high-impact decisions
- Can often be a committee and not a single individual
- Has both veto and approval power

Your Goals:
- Find Decision-Maker early
- Discover Decision-Maker's concerns and goals for their business
- Demonstrate how your solution helps meet business goals

3. Trusted Advisor

Role:
- Protects the Decision-Maker from making a bad decision

Potential Drivers:
- Contribution to Decision-Maker's success
- Enhance personal credibility

Attributes:
- Could be inside or outside the organization
- Could be hidden to others in the organization
- Opinion is highly valued by the Decision-Maker
- Has veto power

Your Goals:
- Find Trusted Advisor early
- Show how supporting your solution will enhance his/her credibility
- Demonstrate how your solution helps meet business goals

4. Specialist

Role:

- Screens out unacceptable proposals
- Judges quantifiable aspects of proposals
- Makes recommendations

Potential Drivers:

- Specifications of exact needs of organization
- Conformity to specifications

Attributes:

- Often says no
- Often tries to convince you he or she is the Decision-Maker
- Often acts as a shield for Decision-Maker
- Can be hidden ... but always exists

Your Goals:

- Learn and/or influence specifications early
- Learn what all the screening tests will be
- Demonstrate how your solution meets or exceeds specifications

5. Utilizer

Role:

- Directly handles or directly supervises those handling your product or service
- Makes judgments about impact on job performance of your product or service
- Often plays another role in addition to Utilizer

Potential Drivers:

- Personal (lives with your product or service)
- Utility, ease of use, efficacy, will it work?

Attributes:

- Rarely a single individual; often a group of people, or pilot group
- Can veto sale
- Will have subjective reactions
- Can sabotage sale if ignored

Your Goals:

- Focus on benefits of your product or service, not cost or features
- Find ways to include Utilizer in developing solution/proposal
- Demonstrate how Utilizer wins by using your solution

6. Gatekeeper

Role:

- Maintain control of the access to decision-maker or others who can impact the decision
- Manage vendors during the decision process

Potential Drivers:

- Control vendors
- Protect others
- Manage the process

Attributes:

- Often the purchasing department or someone playing the purchasing role
- Tend to be lower-level people who are protecting their turf or position
- May or may not play an influencing role

Your Goals:

- Comply with process requests of a Gatekeeper – they can, in some instances, quash your proposal
- Circumvent Gatekeeper through early relation-ship-building with others in the decision process

7. Advocate

Role:

- Acts as your guide in a sale
- Provides important infor-mation which is unavailable through other means

Potential Drivers:

- Influencing the buying deci-sion
- Seeing your proposal succeed

Attributes:

- Must have credibility and/or clout within buying organization
- May be an influencer, but not necessarily
- Must want you to succeed
- Is probably very persuasive
- Knows informal (political) system as well as formal chains of command
- There may be several advocates per sale

Your Goals:

- Enlisting an advocate or advo-cates early in the process
- Continue to nurture relation-ship
- Be on guard for signals that you may be dealing with a "False Advocate"
- In large accounts, try to devel-op more than one advocate

How can you identify these people beyond assessing the attributes listed above? **The Decision Role Identification Tool** can assist you. As you look at the influencers of the key decision-maker, determine the roles they play by answering the questions and determining how many "yes" answers you get. Remember: This is just a tool to help guide you in determining the role the influencer plays. The tool is not perfect nor definitive, but it may point you in the right direction. Many times, this tool is best used with input from a known advocate.

Decision Role Identification Tool

High ranking job or office?	Makes strategic decisions affecting organization?	Has veto and approval power?	Concerned with profits, growth, strategy?	**Executive Approver**
Yes/No	Yes/No	Yes/No	Yes/No	
Can make decision alone?	Gives final approval?	Can change budget?	Concerned with ROI?	**Decision-Maker**
Yes/No	Yes/No	Yes/No	Yes/No	
Is this person external consultant working with Decision-Maker?	Others in organization say this person is close to Decision-Maker?	Is concerned about Decision-Maker's success?	Opinion is highly valued by Decision-Maker?	**Trusted Advisor**
Yes/No	Yes/No	Yes/No	Yes/No	
Has high concern for specifications/ quantifiables of your solution?	Tries to prevent you from contacting others in organization?	Interacts with a lot of management as part of job?	Is concerned with conformity to specifications?	**Specialist**
Yes/No	Yes/No	Yes/No	Yes/No	
Will be affected by implementation of your solution?	Has subjective reactions to your solution?	Makes judgement on impact of job performance due to your solution?	Concerned with utility, ease of use, efficacy of your solution?	**Utilizer**
Yes/No	Yes/No	Yes/No	Yes/No	
Blocks access to key people?	Attempts to control all activity by insisting it run through them?	Lower-level personnel that protects "turf"?	Managed vendors during the decision process?	**Gatekeeper**
Yes/No	Yes/No	Yes/No	Yes/No	
Guides you in making the sale?	Provides feedback/ information important to your success?	Has credibility and clout?	Knows informal (political) system?	**Advocate**
Yes/No	Yes/No	Yes/No	Yes/No	

Now that you have identified the role each of the influencers plays in the decision-making process, let's look at the remaining steps to create an influence map.

To do that, you:

1. Examine your business objective for the organization/department.

2. Identify the decisions that lead to this objective being accomplished and the decision-maker who makes them.

3. Map all the people who influence the decision-maker on EACH decision and their role in the decision-making process.

4. Prioritize this list of influencers based on a composite of their ability to influence the key decision-maker and your ease of accessing them.

5. Examine your network to determine if you know someone who knows one of the influencers.

6. Develop strategies and tactics.

    Let's take a closer look at step 4. Go back to the influence map you drew:

    - Examine the influencers you listed. Think about the level of influence the person has with the key decision-maker and your ability to access each influencer.

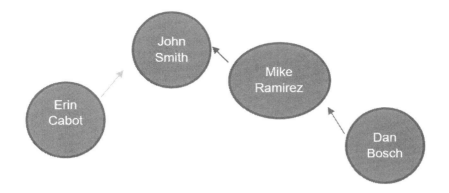

Alter the color of the arrow based on the following:

- Green: High level of influence, high level of accessibility.
- Blue: High level of influence, low level of accessibility.
- Yellow: Low level of influence, high level of accessibility.
- Red: Low level of influence, low level of accessibility.

Once you have prioritized the influencers, you are able to examine your network and determine if you know anyone who can assist you with accessing the influencers of the key decision-maker. This process also allows you to become much more specific in the strategies and tactics you develop, as you can now incorporate ways you will influence the key decision-maker. This can only increase your ability to broaden and deepen your position within the organization/department.

BY TAKING VERY DELIBERATE STEPS AND THINKING THROUGH THE ROLES PEOPLE PLAY IN YOUR ACCOUNT, YOU EVENTUALLY END UP WITH AN ACCOUNT STRATEGY! NOW, YOU WILL NEED TO GO THROUGH THE PROCESS OF FOLLOWING THAT STRATEGY. REMEMBER THAT THIS PROCESS, ALTHOUGH EFFECTIVE, TAKES TIME AND PATIENCE!

Although tired, Sam looked up from his computer and thought: "I know that I can do this! This chapter really helped me in understanding what I have to and how to do it." Before stopping for the night, he once again pulled out his notebook and began writing some key takeaways from this chapter. He wrote:

KEY TAKEAWAYS:

Creating an influence map will help you broaden, deepen and strengthen relationships throughout the organization/department.

Prioritize this list of influencers based on a composite of their ability to influence the key decision-maker and your ease of accessing them.

There are seven decision process roles:
- Executive Approver.
- Decision-Maker.
- Trusted Advisor.
- Specialist.
- Utilizer.
- Gatekeeper.
- Advocate.

Using this process helps you develop an account strategy!

Chapter 5 Check-in Questions

1. **Which of the following is the primary benefit of broadening and strengthening your relationships throughout an organization/department?**
   a. Makes you more knowledgeable than your competitors
   b. Allows you to refer to the Executives you know when dealing
      with lower-level personnel
   c. Have more people in the company who like you
   d. Makes it more likely that you will compete on the business
      value you add rather than on price

2. **Which of the following describes the "decision-maker" role?**
   a. Makes policy decisions
   b. Could be hidden to others in the organization
   c. Has both veto and approval authority
   d. Judges quantifiable aspects of proposals

3. **Which of the following roles screens out unacceptable proposals?**
   a. The executive approver
   b. The specialist
   c. The decision-maker
   d. The trusted advisor

4. **Which of the following roles is most likely to make judgments about whether your product or service will have an impact on job performance?**
   a. The specialist
   b. The decision-maker
   c. The trusted advisor

d. The utilizer

5. Which of the following is the best strategy for "gatekeepers"?
a. Circumvent them through early relationship-building with others
   in the decision process
b. Contact them first to demonstrate the business value of your
   product or service
c. Ask what you can do for them to gain their support
d. Use them to gain access to key persons in the decision
process

6. Which of the following roles acts as a guide during the sale?
a. The specialist
b. The gatekeeper
c. The utilizer
d. The advocate

7. What two measures are used to prioritize influencers?
a. Power and access
b. Influence and position
c. Access and influence
d. Position and access

- To check your answers, turn to page 121.

CHAPTER 6

Creating a Value Proposition

Sam noticed that he was near the end of the materials Doug had sent him. He wanted to finish reading now, but today was a workday so he turned off his computer and headed for his first appointment of the day.

Returning home after 6 that night, Sam put the down the sandwich he had bought on the way home, grabbed a cold drink from the fridge and opened his computer. He was excited about finishing this last chapter and then starting on his account planning for Path International. He began reading:

Just like in the more traditional sales process, you must present a value proposition to your customer. However, the relevant value sought by an Executive is not quality, cost or delivery. Executives and Senior Managers are looking for how you and your company can connect to and support their agenda, issues and initiatives. In contrast, your value proposition for your broader and deeper customers may focus on quality, cost or delivery.

Keep in mind that a value proposition is different from a value statement, in that a value statement communicates the benefits your company offers that are generally applicable to all customers.

The value proposition is:
- Customized to address the needs of a targeted customer within the organization/department.

- Delivers a satisfying outcome to that customer.
- Recognized as superior to alternatives.
- Valued by both you and the customer.
- Clearly stated in value terms.

THE VALUE PROPOSITION IS THE ULTIMATE REASON THAT THE CUSTOMER WILL DECIDE TO WORK WITH YOU AND YOUR ORGANIZATION. YOUR VALUE PROPOSITION IS SPECIFIC AND COMMITS YOUR CLOSING POINTS TO THE CUSTOMER!

This is why your research and your in-depth knowledge of the organization/department is so critical; it is almost impossible to create a true value proposition without it.

DELIVERING VALUE

In a recent study by Bain & Company, 375 companies were asked if they believed they delivered a "superior value proposition" to their clients...

80% of the companies said YES.

Bain then asked the clients of those same companies if they agreed. **Only 8% did!**

So, what is a value proposition?

The sum of all the value of your solution minus the sum of all the costs equals the value proposition.

What is a Value Proposition?

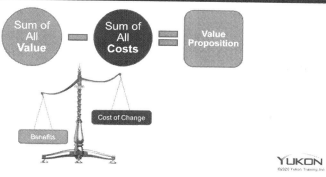

That seems straightforward enough, but there are a couple of questions you need to answer before developing a value proposition:

- Do you clearly know ALL of the value you bring to the table?
- Do you understand ALL of the costs from the customer's perspective, including the cost of change? If not, you may be presenting a value proposition that you think is positive and the customer perceives as negative. No one moves forward if they perceive the costs outweigh the benefits.

We've all done presentations to customers where we looked at the people on the other side of the table and knew they could not care less about what we were talking about. We may have felt we were delivering a dazzling presentation, but it clearly was not resonating with the customer. This may be because we:

- We were not communicating our value in terms that related to the customer.
- Did not understand all of the cost from the customer's perspective.
- If you are presenting a contract and your customer turns right to the financial section to see how much it will cost, or if one of their first questions is "How much will this cost me?," you have not established value.

When we talk about value, we are talking about much more than the products or services you sell. We are talking about everything your company brings to the table that could be a benefit to the customer, including:

- Your programs.
- Your support.
- Your business approach.
- Your responsiveness.
- Your team.
- Your experience and you as their sales professional.

When we talk about cost, we often think of cost as price when really it is everything the customer incurs due to change; it's the cost of change. We might be talking about our price competitiveness in the marketplace, but the customer may be thinking about everything the company would have to do in order to bring in your solution — allocation of resources, training, procedural changes, etc. Therefore, having a thorough understanding of the issues that fall under the cost of change category will be critical to your value proposition.

If the customer perceives that the cost of change will be more than the value of your solution, you end up with a negative value proposition — and no customer will buy from you if that is their perception. So, your value proposition needs to take into consideration all of the things related to the cost of change from the customer's perspective, as well as those elements of value that you and your organization bring to the table that the customer also sees as valuable.

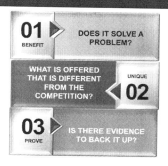

To ensure your value proposition is effective make sure it:

Benefits the customer

It is Unique

You can Prove it

Guidelines for Writing a Value Proposition:

1. Write it from **their** perspective: what will **THEY** get and what are the costs?
2. Use the **customer's** method of **cost justification**.
3. Use the **customer's figures** and **vocabulary**.
4. Consider **all** the **customer's costs**.
5. Consider the **customer's risks**.
6. Anticipate **their questions**.

Below is an example template you can use to help you form your value proposition:

The Value Proposition (concise, clear, relative to a specific offering)	
Customer Name:	ABC Consumer Products, Inc.
... will be able to improve what (the problem)?	Will be able to reduce the time that your salesforce spends out of the field while learning new skills
... by how much?	By an average of 1-2 days per session
... through the ability to do what?	Through the use of our unique "Surround the Classroom" approach developed by Yukon Training which involves pre, post and follow-up online programs designed specifically for busy salespeople
... as a result of which of your company's solution offerings?	Which will reduce costs and increase efficiency in the classroom and in the field
... over what period of time or by when?	Over the next 12 months and 3 days of classroom work per person
... at a cost of?	Reducing your overall (internal and external) cost per session by $2,700 per person
... which will provide a positive quantifiable outcome of xxx?	Providing an annualized savings for your 500 salespeople of over $1.3 million!

VALUE PROPOSITION EXAMPLE TO SENIOR SALES MANAGER WITH 500 SALESPEOPLE

ABC Consumer Products, Inc. will be able to reduce the time it takes to enhance skills of your salespeople an average of 3 days through the use of a customized and unique "Surround the Classroom" system. Developed by Yukon Training, this involves pre, post and follow-up online programs designed specifically for busy salespeople and will reduce costs and increase efficiencies both in live and online training at an overall cost reduction of $2,700 per person, providing an annualized savings of over $1.3 million.

Your ability to tailor your value proposition to the customer's needs increases your ability to create a compelling reason to move forward and supplies the proof that you have been listening to their needs and are focused on helping them succeed. By providing a financially oriented value proposition including specific numbers or percentages, you "speak" to Executives and Senior Managers and get their attention faster. With today's tight economy and overburdened decision-makers, you need to have a strong value proposition to cut through the clutter and get their attention. A customized, financially driven value proposition communicated effectively will improve your ability to reach an agreement and gain commitment for the sale!

Your value proposition should change from customer to customer, from account to account. Sales needs to value something different than finance. Marketing needs to value something different than procurement.

Here are a few examples of value propositions from some of our customers (names and products have been changed to protect their identities).

(Major Consumer Products Company, Senior VP Sales) DEP, Inc. will be able to drive additional incremental sales at 5 key retailers by $40 million through expanding investment in retail coverage to maximize in store programs, maintain distribution and improve on shelf over the next six months, which will drive a 8:1 return on a $5 million investment and enable DEP, Inc. to meet our year-end sales goal!

(Pharmaceutical company speaking to a large medical facility) At ABC Pharma, we can help you with the number of call backs from patients asking for help with their prescriptions. Many of our customers have seen the number of call backs reduced by over 50%! By sending the prescriptions through our specialized call center while the patient is still here with you, your patients can get their prescriptions within 48 hours with a lower copay that will greatly reduce your call backs from both pharmacists and patients! The only cost to you would be the time it takes over lunch to educate the staff. What would it mean to you and your staff to be able to take a lunch break and leave on time?

(Salesperson to Retail Store Buyer) AAA will be able to increase your sales by an incremental $1.5 million and be the retailer of choice for consumers dealing with colds during the month of February by creating a unique campaign at no cost to AAA featuring MirraCure, the number one brand in fighting colds. How does that sound?

(Salesperson speaking with a Medical Oncologist)
Dr., we understand that you are looking for more treatment

options for your patients with advanced disease state. XXX is an additional therapy at your disposal to treat these patients due to its unique properties that will NOT add to severe life-threatening skeletal issues that other radiopharmaceutical agents can. This, then, provides an overall survival benefit to your patients without compromising your ability to use chemotherapy and other pharmaceuticals. How could that benefit your patients?

Sam wrote the following notes in his expanding account notebook:

KEY TAKEAWAYS:
- The value proposition:
  - Is customized to address the needs of a targeted customer within the organization/department.
  - Delivers a satisfying outcome to that customer.
  - Is recognized as superior to alternatives.
  - Is valued by both you and the customer.
  - Is clearly stated in value terms.
- The sum of all the value of your solution minus the sum of all the costs equals the value proposition.
  - Value is more than products and service you sell. Value can be found in the following: Your programs, your support, your business approach, your responsiveness, your team and you as a sales professional.
- Cost is everything a customer incurs due to change.
- Your value proposition needs to take into consideration the cost of change to the customer as well as the value you and your organization bring.
- Effective value propositions:
  - Benefits.

- ○ Is Unique.
- ○ You can Prove.
- Guidelines for Writing a Value Proposition:
  - ○ Write it from their perspective: What will THEY get and what are the costs?
  - ○ Use the customer's method of cost justification.
  - ○ Use the customer's figures and vocabulary.
  - ○ Consider all the customer's costs.
  - ○ Consider the customer's risks.
  - ○ Anticipate their questions.

Chapter 6 Check-in Questions

1. **Which of the following describes a value proposition?**
   a. It solves all of the customer's major problems
   b. It is customized and recognized as a superior alternative
   c. It states at least one creative idea for doing something differently
   d. Both b and c

2. **What must an effective value proposition do for a customer?**
   a. Exceptional, Essential, Exciting
   b. Benefit, Unique, Prove
   c. Achievable, Believable, Conceivable
   d. Connect, Contrast, Confirm

3. **Which of the following is a guideline for writing a value proposition?**
   a. Write it from their perspective
   b. Use your company's method of cost justification
   c. Do not include risks to the customer
   d. Use vocabulary familiar to you

4. **Which of the following is an advantage of including numbers and/or percentages in your value proposition?**
   a. It lets the customer know that you have put a lot of effort into creating the value proposition
   b. It allows the customer to compare your solution to others
   c. It lets the customer know that you are familiar with financial matters
   d. It "speaks" to Executives and Senior Managers and gains their attention

- To check your answers, turn to page 121.

CHAPTER 7

Final Thoughts

After writing his notes in his account notebook, Sam sat back and reflected on all the material he had read and studied over the last couple of weeks. He was amazed that previously, he had only thought about implementing just a few of the numerous suggestions that he had just learned about in the materials from Doug. "Wow," he thought, "had I been exposed to even a small portion of this earlier in my sales career, I might be making a lot more money now!" After a chuckle, he remembered that even though he had been in sales for almost 5 years, he really was a novice and had just recently started to feel more comfortable in his sales role. "But now," he thought, "I can 'ring the bell' a lot more and make a real difference." He got up from his desk and headed to his freezer. Opening the freezer, he reached in for a pint of rocky road ice cream and began thinking of how he was going to get to the highest level of managers in Path International. His mind was swirling with ideas as he plunged his spoon into that frozen treat!

Subject: Many Thanks!

Doug:

I have finished the materials and I owe you a big favor! How about meeting me tomorrow after work at Harry's Pub on Main Street at 5:30? Drinks and dinner are on me! I'm really excited about how I can develop these skills I have learned in the materials.

All my best!

Sam

As he was getting into bed, he thought, "This is going to be a lot of work, but I can already visualize my boss, Victoria, handing me the 'Salesperson of the Year' trophy next year! And when I speak with Victoria tomorrow, I believe that she will see that I'm ready to make a dazzling report to Devin West, the new VP of Sales! Yep, things are really looking up!"

What Senior Executives Want Salespeople to Know

PURPOSE OF THIS RESEARCH

This white paper presents the most relevant findings of an intensive research project designed to explore the role that senior executives play in the strategic procurement process and to better understand their expectations of sales professionals involved in those projects. The study was conducted by Yukon Training, Inc. in concert with Virginia Tech.

In the past twenty years, there have been a number of similar studies conducted by other organizations seeking to examine the executive's role in the strategic buying process. One such interview-based study that is referenced in this paper and often cited in corporate education for sales professionals was conducted by Target Marketing in 1996.[1]

OUR APPROACH

This study began in November 2009 with quantitative research conducted by Virginia Tech, led by Kent Nakamoto, Ph.D. and Donna C. Wertalik. To reduce bias and maintain objectivity, the study was designed with both quantitative and qualitative components. The first phase consisted of an online survey instrument that was sent out via email to more than 8,000 senior executives in the United States across a wide variety of industries.

Based on industry benchmarks, we expected a response rate of around 2% for this audience, or 160 responses. The number of responses achieved was slightly lower at 131.

There were a wide variety of industries represented including government, private and non-profit organizations. Some demographic highlights from the respondents in this study include the following:

- 76% were C-level officers in their organization
- 63% had division/company sales of more than $100M
- 33% agreed to participate in interviews

The second phase of the study consisted of follow-up interviews with those executives indicating a willingness to participate in a 15-20 minute conversation. These interviews were conducted by members of the Pi Sigma Epsilon fraternity, a professional sales and marketing organization at Virginia Tech, along with several executives from Yukon. The focus of these interviews was to expand on key themes within the quantitative data and to identify additional insight into their role in the procurement process.

INVOLVEMENT LEVELS INCREASING

When asked whether their activity level in strategic purchases will change over the next six months, 86% of the respondents said their level of involvement would either increase or remain the same, leaving only 14% who anticipate a reduced role in the process.

EXECUTIVES GET INVOLVED EARLY

When asked what their involvement was in the strategic purchase decision, executives indicated their highest level of participation was early in the purchasing process. Their focus centered on "Understanding current issues" and "Setting overall strategy." In the middle of the purchase decision, where vendor selection occurs, executives had the least involvement, spending most of their time overseeing delegated tasks.

Q. WHAT BEST DESCRIBES YOUR INVOLVEMENT IN MAJOR PURCHASING DECISIONS?

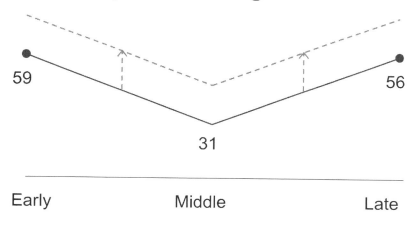

Executive Involvement In Major Purchasing Decisions

59

31

56

Early   Middle   Late

SO GIVEN THE CHOICE, WHERE IS IT BEST FOR SALESPEOPLE TO ENTER THE PROCESS?

Well, let's start with where it is easiest … that's in the middle. But there are daunting challenges with this approach. First, executive involvement is lowest during this stage of the process, with vendor selection delegated to others. And in many organizations, this is the point where the formalprocur ement process starts, thereby limiting access to executive stakeholders and funneling all communication through a single point of contact within procurement.

Salespeople could also choose to wait until later in the process when the executive reappears. But by the time this happens, selection criteria have been firmly established and the list of potential candidates narrowed to only a select few that have been vetted along the way.

That leaves the early stage of the process as clearly the best option. There are several reasons for this. First, in the very early stages of the process, executives are more receptive to learning about the potential value a new partner could bring to the table. For the executive, the risk is low and the reward potentially high. Second, it is in this stage that objectives are established and an overall strategy is developed. Getting "plugged in" to the executive at this point can give sales professionals the ability to help influence and shape thinking around these critical items. Finally, this stage is also where the procurement process begins taking shape, making access to executives and other key stakeholders a little easier.

The "V" shape of the curve shown is consistent with the results obtained in similar studies. To enable a more direct comparison to the results from the 1996 Target Marketing study, we included a companion question on participation in specific activities related to these three stages of the purchasing process.

Q. IN ADVANCE OF INITIATING A MAJOR PURCHASE DECISION, WHICH OF THE FOLLOWING ARE YOU MOST LIKELY TO DEVOTE TIME TO?

Stage	Item	Percentage
Early	Understanding current issues involved in the decision	65%
Early	Establishing objectives to be met when making the decision	50%
Early	Setting overall strategy	65%
Middle	Exploring options for completing tasks	19%
Middle	Setting criteria for evaluating vendors	27%
Middle	Examining alternative solutions to current plans	31%
Late	Planning the implementation of the project	19%
Late	Measuring results	45%

The general distribution of these results mirror those found in the Target Marketing study. The only significant difference appeared to be with regard to planning and implementation. When asked about this during the qualitative portion of our research, a majority of executives said that they did not get involved much with planning the project's implementation, more often choosing to delegate such tasks.

*The increasing popularity of business networking tools such as LinkedIn®
has made it easier to connect with potential referral sources. But according
to our research, sales professionals could find this to be an ineffective way to
connect directly with an executive.*

*Based on our interviews, networking tools are more effective when utilized
as a way to get introduced to, and stay in touch with, company employees
and other industry professionals who might in the future provide a referral to
a targeted executive.*

INDIRECT APPROACH TO ACCESS PAYS DIVIDENDS

When asked what channels of communication were most effective in
reaching them, a majority of executives indicated that a referral from
someone inside their company was most effective. Referrals from an
outside source were second on their list.

Q. WHAT CHANNELS OF COMMUNICATION ARE MOST EFFECTIVE IN GAINING ACCESS TO YOU?

Rate each channel on a scale from 1 (not effective) to 5 (very
effective)

Item	1	2	3	4	5	Mean
Referral from inside source	4	3	11	39	74	4.34
Referral from outside source	7	6	20	76	22	3.76
Email followed by phone call	19	15	31	53	13	3.20
Direct phone call	25	28	34	27	17	2.87
Written letter followed by phone call	18	35	35	33	10	2.86
Social media groups (Linkedin, etc)	41	19	46	16	9	2.49

Over 86% of the executives we surveyed rated a referral from an inside source as an effective method for gaining access to them, with a full 56% of the total population rating this method as very effective. Executives place more trust and credibility in the recommendations of others inside the organization. This single finding makes the case for building a broad network of relationships inside the client organization as a path toward meeting with senior executives inside the company.

Recommendations from individuals outside the organization also scored high, with 75% of executives rating that method as effective. The number of individuals rating it as very effective, however, was lower than for internal referrals (17%).

During our interviews, there was a lot of discussion about the method of "cold calling." Much of this discussion was initiated by the executive without prompting. While the overall mean response was not high (33% rating it as effective), responses to the effectiveness of direct phone calls were fairly evenly distributed across the rating scale. Effectiveness of this method as a whole was significantly higher than in previous research.

FIRST IMPRESSIONS STILL MATTER

While a professional appearance scored lower than some of the other differentiators on our list, it is important not to dismiss its importance. When asked, most of the executives we interviewed felt that a professional appearance was more requirement than differentiator.

In fact, some of the executives that we spoke with pointed out that a poor or unprofessional appearance would definitely differentiate the salesperson from his peers... just not in the way that the salesperson had hoped.

RESPONSIVENESS REIGNS ... IT'S NOT ABOUT YOU

When asked to identify the best way for a salesperson to differentiate himself or herself from others, the two highest ranking responses were "Listening before proposing a solution" and "Responsiveness to my requests and questions." While most sales professionals will tell you that listening is a fundamental selling skill, it is even more important for the salesperson to demonstrate both an ability and a willingness to really listen while on an executive call.

Q. ONCE BEING GRANTED A MEETING WITH YOU, WHAT IS THE BEST WAY FOR A SALESPERSON TO DIFFERENTIATE HIMSELF OR HERSELF?

Rate each channel on a scale from 1 (not effective) to 5 (very effective)

Item	1	2	3	4	5	Mean
Responsiveness to your requests and questions	5	2	19	35	70	4.38
Ability to provide accurate comparison of capabilities to goals	6	6	11	45	63	4.17
Thorough understanding of business environments and markets	6	5	16	47	57	4.10
Track record of accomplishments within your industry	4	4	32	56	35	3.87
Professional presentation and materials	5	3	30	64	29	3.83
Apparent authority within his/her own company	9	7	32	56	27	3.65
Professional appearance	8	4	41	64	14	3.55

One of the worst things a salesperson can do when meeting with a senior executive is to focus more on the specifics of their products and services at the expense of a discussion focused on industry- or business-specific initiatives and issues. This tendency was cited by many executives as a common mistake and one that is difficult for the salesperson to overcome.

Just like in the more traditional sales process, you must present a value proposition to the executive. But the relevant value sought by an executive is not quality, cost or delivery. Executives are looking for how you and your company can connect to and support their agenda, issues and initiatives.

IF YOU WANT TO GET ASKED BACK

We asked executives to select the most important quality a salesperson can demonstrate to receive first consideration for future business. Their top responses, and the percentage of times each was selected as most important, were:

- Responsiveness to critical issues (42%)
- Trust developed, sharing similar goals/values (25%)
- Deep understanding of industry and future insights (14%)
- Flexibility and willingness to work well within the executive organization (9%)

This finding, coupled with results of the previous question, gives a clear mandate to the salesperson who wants to be successful when working with executives – responsiveness is paramount to your success … on the first as well as future projects.

COMMUNICATION - KEY TO AN ONGOING RELATIONSHIP

Sales professionals know the importance of keeping their clients informed. But while executives want to be kept informed, they don't want a salesperson calling them several times a day. Salespeople should be able to determine what items an executive would want to be informed of and contact them only when it's appropriate.

In a recent article by McKinsey & Company, they shared the results of a survey of more than 1,200 purchasing decision makers in small, medium and large size companies throughout the United States and Western Europe. When asked to identify a given selling activity that was "most destructive" to the sales experience, 35% of the respondents selected "too much contact – in person, by phone or via email."[2] When communicating with an executive in that all-important first meeting, executives want you to:

- Have done your "homework" prior to the meeting
- Leave the PowerPoint slides at home
- Connect your message to their strategy and initiatives
- Make your point early in the discussion

TREAD LIGHTLY

Several executives recounted stories of bright, young sales professionals who did and said all the right things to pique the executive's interest, land the initial meeting and obtain the right to be heard by relevant members of the executive's team ... only to eliminate any chance of working with the executive's organization through too frequent and irrelevant communication and contact with the executive.

EXECUTIVES TAKE A HANDS-ON APPROACH TO RESEARCH

When asked how they seek information on potential vendors, almost every executive in our survey said that they used the Internet in one way or another (93%). Executives indicated they were looking for information on the salesperson, the company they represented, or in many cases, both.

Our results align with research conducted by Google on the use of the Internet by C-suite executives. Their assessment of Fortune 500 executives at companies with revenues exceeding $1B annually showed that 73% are using the Internet daily and further that 64% conduct six or more searches each day to locate business information.[3] Forbes and Gartner assert that the Internet continues to be the most influential and important source of business information for C-Level executives around the world, at 67%.[4]

SITES THEY VISIT AND TOOLS THEY USE TO CONDUCT RESEARCH INCLUDE:

- Google (www.google.com)
- Hoover's (www.hoovers.com)
- LinkedIn (www.linkedin.com)
- Dunn and Bradstreet (www.dnb.com)
- OneSource (www.onesource.com)

Several executives in our survey expressed a very deliberate approach in using the Internet to evaluate a salesperson and their organization prior to agreeing to the initial meeting. This underscores the importance of being aware of what information is out there on the Internet about your company. This awareness starts with, but is not limited to, your company's own website.

You should also be "listening" to what others might be saying about you and your company. In addition to subscribing to RSS feeds via tools like Google Reader, other popular tools that executives use to listen to what others are saying online include:

- Google Alerts (www.alerts.google.com)
- Technorati (www.technorati.com)
- Twitter (www.searchtwitter.com)
- Blog Pulse (www.blogpulse.com)
- Board Tracker (www.boardtracker.com)

SUMMARY AND CONCLUSIONS

This nationwide study highlights the role that senior executives play in the strategic procurement process in a wide variety of industries and outlines their expectations of sales professionals. Key findings of this study include:

With regard to involvement of the senior executive in the strategic procurement process, we found that

- Most are involved in the early stages where strategy is developed and objectives established.
- They are least involved in the middle stages where more task-related work is delegated to others.
- Involvement is also strong at the later stages of the process, particularly when it comes to measurement of results.

We also found that

- Based on current economic conditions, executive involvement in strategic purchases will increase in the coming months.
- The most effective way to gain access to an executive continues

to be through a referral from someone inside the executive's own organization. A referral from someone outside the organization is the second most effective means of gaining access.

- Responsiveness to questions and requests from executives is the most effective way for a salesperson to differentiate themselves.
- Communication with executives and other key stakeholders throughout the procurement process can lead to strong consideration for future business, but only if handled appropriately.
- Executives are actively using the Internet to research individuals and companies before agreeing to an initial meeting.

REFERENCES

[1]Gardner, A., Bistritz, S., and Klompmaker, J. (1996). Selling to Senior Executives: How salespeople establish trust and credibility with senior executives. [Target Marketing Systems, White paper].

[2]Boaz, N., Murnane, J., and Nuffer, K. (2010). The basics of business-to-business sales success. McKinsey Quarterly. Retrieved from http://www.mckinseyquarterly.com/ The_basics_of_business-to-business_sales_success_2586

[3]Booker, E. (2009). Google unveils research on executive Internet use. BtoB Magazine. Retrieved from http://www.btobonline.com/apps/pbcs.dll/ article?AID=2009906129979

[4]Scharler, M. (2008). Forbes.com and Gartner Study Reveals a 37% Increase in C-Level Executives Who Choose the Internet as their No. 1 Source of Business Information.
Forbes.com. Retrieved from http://www.forbesinc.com/newsroom/releases/ forbescom/FDCCLevelStudy062408.pdf

ABOUT THE AUTHORS

Chris Ayers is the President and CEO of Yukon Group, Inc. Chris has over 25 years of experience in sales, operations and organizational development. Chris has a B.S. in Mathematics from Shenandoah University and an MBA from Virginia Commonwealth University.

Brian Collins is a Senior Vice-President with Yukon Group, Inc. and heads up their sales organization. Brian has over 20 years of sales experience and has spent most of his career in the financial services arena. Brian holds a B.S. in Finance and a MBA in Finance from Virginia Tech.

Kent Nakamoto is the R.B. Pamplin Professor of Marketing, Head of the Department of Marketing, and Associate Dean for Research in the Pamplin College of Business at Virginia Tech. He holds a B.S. in chemistry from the California Institute of Technology, M.A. in Arts Administration and M.S. in Marketing from the University of Wisconsin-Madison, and Ph.D. in business from Stanford University.

Donna Wertalik has more than 18 years of sales and marketing experience working for Fortune 500 companies as well as several leading New York- based advertising agencies. Donna holds a B.S. in Marketing from Fairleigh Dickinson University and a MBA from Columbia College and is a Marketing Instructor at Virginia Tech.

APPENDIX II

ELEVATOR SPEECH EXAMPLES

What do you say when you only have a few seconds to make an impression or you have to leave a message that will lead to another opportunity to speak? Here are some "generic" examples:

We help our retail customers improve the lives of their consumers and patients as well as increase their profits. We are unique in that we have products that benefit people during every life stage — from conception to end of life. I work for ABC Consumer, Inc. We bring research to life every day through the products we sell. How important is health to you?

We work with hospitals and oncology clinics to help them offer an innovative biologic to patients dealing with life-threatening disease and bring hope to patients with cancer. We are unique in that we offer a high-quality product with generous patient support services at a discounted price. How important is high quality at lower cost in your pharmacy?

I work with developers to create and construct exceptional properties across many top brands. Our team of dedicated experts and professionals support our development partners and franchisees every step of the way. From design and construction to opening, and ongoing operations, XYZ offers access to the latest tools, technology and innovative solutions that deliver bottom line results to owners by driving guest stays, enhancing guest experience and creating more efficient hotel operations. Does being a part of the leading and largest hotel franchise company interest you?

We, as you do, work with a unique set of patients to help them manage all their difficult symptoms and help them stabilize their lives so they can once again function normally. What would it mean to you to help your patients gain their lives back?

KEY TAKEAWAYS

This book has provided you information and skill sets that will allow you to:

- Analyze a customer's business to identify their business needs, concerns, challenges and goals.
- Provide information and products in a way that will develop partnerships by incorporating customer needs.
- Gain access to all levels of an organization by using indirect approaches.
- Conduct meetings that will result in increased business.
- Develop a value proposition that provides customers with a reason to buy from you.
- Broaden and deepen your connections by determining the influencers of a decision within an organization or department, using influence maps.

Yes, selling is difficult — but by using proven techniques from others and applying yourself to any of the many challenges salespeople face, you can be even more successful!

Check-in Questions – Answer Key

Chapter 1:
1. D
2. A
3. C
4. B

Chapter 2:
1. C
2. B
3. D
4. B
5. D

Chapter 3:
1. C
2. A
3. D
4. B

Chapter 4:
1. D
2. A
3. C
4. D
5. B

Chapter 5:
1. D
2. C
3. B
4. D
5. A
6. D
7. C

Chapter 6:
1. B
2. B
3. A
4. D

About Yukon Training

Yukon is a global training partner with experience training professionals on six continents. We are proud that over 86% of our clients are repeat business and more than 77% are referrals. We have had the pleasure of training over 140,000 professionals.

PRACTICAL SALES AND SALES TRAINING EXPERIENCE

Our instructors are more than facilitators. They have extensive experience and possess the ability to call upon skills to assist participants with real-life scenarios.

COMMITMENT TO VALUE

At Yukon Training we are strong believers in value; it's what we teach! We are committed to quality, fairness and flawless execution. We ensure this by viewing training as more than an event – it is an investment in your team and is achieved when we partner every step of the way.

CUSTOMER INVOLVEMENT – DESIGN AND IMPLEMENTATION TO ACHIEVE RESULTS

There are three very distinct phases of training that make it more than an event: before, during and after. We partner with you in preparing for the event, handling the training program and offering ongoing coaching programs to continue the learning long after the event has concluded.

Our flexibility is unsurpassed in the training world. We work with you to design a training approach that best suits your goals, rather than dictating that our process is the only one that works. We understand that every organization has its own way of operating, and that any training program must be a part of their business culture. We document the steps we take before, during, and after when creating the total design and implementation process.

E-LEARNING

Yukon has developed a suite of e-Learning products that include online modules and Cameo™, Yukon's unique and robust learning reinforcement tool delivered via email.

RESULTS-ORIENTED

Our success is your success. We are proud to conduct our business at the highest level of ethical standards.

YUKON'S INSTRUCTOR-LED COURSES TO ROUND OUT A COMPLETE TRAINING CURRICULUM INCLUDE:

COMMUNICATING WITH CONFIDENCE

CREATING AND COMMUNICATING EFFECTIVE VALUE PROPOSITIONS

CUSTOMER FOCUSED NEGOTIATIONS

HANDLING DIFFICULT NEGOTIATORS

INFLUENCING WITH IMPACT

MASTER ACCOUNT PLANNING

PERSUASIVE PRESENTATION SKILLS

REFLECTIVE LISTENING

SELLING HIGHER, BROADER AND DEEPER

---

www.YukonTraining.com

Made in the USA
Middletown, DE
01 October 2020

20575578R00087